GROWING AN
IN-SYNC
CHILD

GROWING AN IN-SYNC CHILD

Simple, Fun Activities to Help

Every Child

Develop, Learn, and Grow

Carol Kranowitz, M.A.
and
Joye Newman, M.A.

A PERIGEE BOOK

A PERIGEE BOOK
Published by the Penguin Group
Penguin Group (USA) Inc.
375 Hudson Street, New York, New York 10014, USA
Penguin Group (Canada), 90 Eglinton Avenue East, Suite 700, Toronto, Ontario M4P 2Y3, Canada
(a division of Pearson Penguin Canada Inc.)
Penguin Books Ltd., 80 Strand, London WC2R 0RL, England
Penguin Group Ireland, 25 St. Stephen's Green, Dublin 2, Ireland (a division of Penguin Books Ltd.)
Penguin Group (Australia), 250 Camberwell Road, Camberwell, Victoria 3124, Australia
(a division of Pearson Australia Group Pty. Ltd.)
Penguin Books India Pvt. Ltd., 11 Community Centre, Panchsheel Park, New Delhi—110 017, India
Penguin Group (NZ), 67 Apollo Drive, Rosedale, Auckland 0632, New Zealand
(a division of Pearson New Zealand Ltd.)
Penguin Books (South Africa) (Pty.) Ltd., 24 Sturdee Avenue, Rosebank, Johannesburg 2196, South Africa

Penguin Books Ltd., Registered Offices: 80 Strand, London WC2R 0RL, England

While the authors have made every effort to provide accurate telephone numbers, Internet addresses, and other contact information at the time of publication, neither the publisher nor the authors assume any responsibility for errors, or for changes that occur after publication. Further, the publisher does not have any control over and does not assume any responsibility for author or third-party websites or their content.

First edition: May 2010

Library of Congress Cataloging-in-Publication Data

Kranowitz, Carol Stock.
  Growing an in-sync child : simple, fun activities to help every child develop, learn, and grow /
Carol Kranowitz and Joye Newman.
    p. cm.
  Includes index.
  ISBN 978-0-399-53583-3
  1. Motor ability in children. I. Newman, Joye. II. Title.
  RJ133.K73 2010
  612'.04—dc22   2009047639

PRINTED IN THE UNITED STATES OF AMERICA

10 9 8 7 6 5 4

Neither the publisher nor the authors are engaged in rendering professional advice or services to the individual reader. The ideas, procedures, and suggestions contained in this book are not intended as a substitute for consulting with your physician. All matters regarding your health require medical supervision. Neither the authors nor the publisher shall be liable or responsible for any loss or damage allegedly arising from any information or suggestion in this book.

Most Perigee books are available at special quantity discounts for bulk purchases for sales promotions, premiums, fund-raising, or educational use. Special books, or book excerpts, can also be created to fit specific needs. For details, write: Special Markets, Penguin Group (USA) Inc., 375 Hudson Street, New York, New York 10014.

In loving memory of our wise parents,

Betty and Marvin Newman
and
Doris and Herman Stock

Tell me, and I forget. Teach me, and I remember.
Involve me, and I learn.
—BENJAMIN FRANKLIN

A journey of a thousand miles begins with a single step.
—LAO TZU

We want to focus on activity . . . and we want everybody to think
about moving their bodies.
—MICHELLE OBAMA,
2009 White House Easter Egg Roll

You put your right foot in, you put your right foot out . . .
That's what it's all about.
—"THE HOKEY POKEY"

Contents

PART ONE

The Importance of Being In Sync

PART TWO

Getting Started with the In-Sync Program

PART THREE

The In-Sync Activities

Advanced Activities

PART FOUR

Appendices

Many Thanks

We are eternally grateful to many people who helped us grow this book, including:

Larry Paul, who embraces, supports, and delights in Joye and her passion for promoting happy, healthy childhoods.

Mark Zweig, whose mindfulness, wisdom, and loving support of Carol faileth never.

Joye's children, Ami, Miri, and Benjy, for listening to her talk and talk about how much fun she and Carol have had collaborating on this book.

Carol's sons, Jeremy and David, and daughters-in-law, Jenny and Melissa, for listening to her talk and talk about how much fun she and Joye have had collaborating on this book.

Carol's grandchildren, Eden, Aaron, Asher, Noah, and Isaac, for cheerfully trying the activities and offering their own ingenious variations.

Joye's pets, Hailey Sue and Jesse James, for being the most In Sync dog and cat in the world.

Amiel Francke, OD, Joye's mentor extraordinaire, who guides and nurtures her professionally and personally and shares his brilliance about vision and its importance in living an In-Sync life.

The incredibly dedicated and creative staff at Kids Moving Company, who over the years have helped get so many children In Sync.

Wise and wonderful Marguerite Kelly, for generously sharing her knowledge with parents everywhere and for teaching us the art and science of how to get this book into your hands.

The staff at Apple Store Bethesda Row, especially Thom, Kelly-Ann, Pearl, Hugh, Danny, Ned, Paul, Steve, Marcy, and Doug.

Jane Healy, for writing the splendid foreword to this book and for her life's work, which is to get children actively participating in the world around them.

Our illustrator, Durell Godfrey, for her delightful illustrations.

Our Perigee editor, Marian Lizzi, and publisher, John Duff, for their thoughtful guidance and support.

Ethel in Kansas, her In-Sync son, Frankie, and all the other children who accompany us on our journey.

Our beloved parents, guarding us from above, who taught us what we know and how to be.

Most of all, each other, forever.

Joye and Carol
Bethesda, Maryland
Spring 2010

Foreword

WHEN KIDS RUN, catch balls, roll down a hill, splash joyously in puddles without falling down, and relate to others with an easy grace appropriate to their age, they are "strengthening their bodies and brains." These are simple and powerful words from Carol Kranowitz and Joye Newman to describe the child's natural learning curve. Physical activity: It's what kids do, the basic connection that ignites a lifetime of intelligence. Seems obvious, doesn't it? Well, it is—for children who are "In Sync."

As any educator can tell you, children who are not In Sync have always been with us, puzzling and worrying their teachers, psychologists, and—especially—their parents. Currently, pediatricians, teachers, and parents are troubled by a rapid increase in children who have somehow missed out on the body-brain connection and are seriously delayed in basic physical and perceptual skill development.

Professionals attribute this worrisome trend to the altered landscape of twenty-first century childhood—an excess of electronic playtime and screen-time, with a commensurate lack of physical and creative activity. These are natural steps toward integrating body and brain on the way to a fully functioning intellect. Mature thinking and learning are founded on neural pathways that develop as a child masters physical coordination, skilled movement, balance, and many other skills inherent in sensory and perceptual motor development.

Yet our hyper-stressed pursuit of "progress" has convinced many parents and teachers that "child's play" is an outdated waste of time.

"Why should a digital generation spend valuable learning time on rough-and-tumble, gooey, muddy, spontaneous physical fun?" they wonder. There's work to do, academic skills to master, the electronic universe to conquer!

Oh, how wrong they are! It is your child's *active* manipulation of, and response to, the three-dimensional world around her that sets a course for her future intelligence.

Kranowitz and Newman urge us to give the electronic entertainments a rest and resist trying to accelerate learning. Fortunately, they also tell us how to reverse these damaging trends while identifying and targeting any child's specific areas of need. They give us a series of flexible activities that can be adapted to time and place, as well as the child's ability and attention span.

I challenge you to choose a relaxed setting and sample these activities with a child without having fun! Start with the basic ones, and don't be fooled; these seemingly lighthearted games and the authors' easy style belie their profound importance. While you can't yet peer inside a child's brain to observe what is happening when she practices games such as Arm Circles or Paper Plate Play, you can be sure that something important is going on in there.

Hopefully, you will also be willing to act as "guinea pig," try the activities yourself, and even look a little foolish in the process. If so, you will provide a model of not only how to meet a new challenge but also how to relax, laugh, and generate your own fun together rather than having it brought to you by some electronic device.

Thank you, Joye and Carol, for giving us this helpful means of tuning in to body and brain as we work on becoming an In Sync human family.

—JANE M. HEALY, PH.D.,
author of *Your Child's Growing Mind* and *Different Learners*

Introduction

JOYE AND CAROL TAKE A WALK

During a glorious spring walk beside the Potomac River near Washington, DC, we spot a toddler gleefully pushing his stroller along the gravelly path. We watch his mother encourage this heavy-work activity, even though their progress is slow and zigzaggy. "You are so strong!" she says. He looks up at her, giggling, and the stroller lurches off-course toward the bushes. His mother quickly steps in front. "Whoa!" she says. The child stops the stroller in time and, with some effort, corrects his pilot error.

We understand the immense value of this interaction among Mom, child, and stroller. This mother is growing an In-Sync child, and we are delighted!

Around the bend, we see a six-year-old stomping through a puddle and a twelve-year-old balancing on a fallen tree trunk. We know that these active children are strengthening their bodies and brains—much more than many of their peers who are indoors staring at a video screen or being drilled with flash cards.

Such seemingly unremarkable experiences as stomping and balancing can, in fact, be the foundation for optimal physical, academic, social, and emotional growth.

As educators, we worry that we see so few children having these really important movement adventures. We have been walking and talking together for years, sharing our observations of children, brainstorming about solutions to kids' challenges, collaborating on treatment plans, comparing experiences at school and clinic, and discussing research in each of our fields.

On this beautiful day, as we walk, we talk about how maneuvering a stroller can prepare a child for handwriting, how splashing through a puddle can improve attention, and how walking across a tree trunk can enhance vision. We are so happy we have each other because we understand each other's thoughts and speak the same language. We share the same love and passion for children. We agree that sensory and motor experiences are crucial for children's development and learning.

Unfortunately, many parents and educators believe that the earlier a child learns to read and write, the better off he will be. To that end, they provide video and computer programs, paper and pencil games, and other sedentary tasks, hoping to develop the child's academic skills. Parents and teachers may not understand that, for the young child, a walk along the river is a much more developmentally and academically appropriate use of the child's time.

And so, we bemoan the fact that technological advances have usurped the place of simple walks outdoors. We realize that in this out-of-sync world, how to grow an In-Sync child is something every parent and teacher deserves to know. Thus was conceived the book you hold in your hands.

GROWING AN
IN-SYNC
CHILD

PART ONE

The Importance of Being In Sync

The In-Sync Child

▼

ET'S START WITH a quiz on some abilities and behaviors that your child may exhibit in daily life. The list is by no means exhaustive.

DOES YOUR CHILD . . .
- ❑ Move easily and effectively?
- ❑ Enjoy movement?
- ❑ Join in group games?
- ❑ Try new activities?

DOES YOUR CHILD find it easy to . . .
- ❑ Function in a classroom environment?
- ❑ Work well in groups?
- ❑ Make friends?
- ❑ Keep his personal space (cubby, desk, room, locker) organized?
- ❑ Get dressed?

IS YOUR CHILD . . .
- ❑ Emotionally secure?
- ❑ Easy to get along with?
- ❑ Comfortable in the world?

Look at the list above and think about your child. You can probably check at least one behavior in each group. The more checks there are, the more likely it is that your child is "In Sync."

When you are In Sync, your movements are efficient and fluid. You feel comfortable in your body, and when you are comfortable in your body, you feel good. When you feel good, you function better. Everything works.

In a perfect world, we would all be In Sync all the time. In a perfect world, we would be less sedentary. We would walk where we needed to go rather than drive. In our own gardens, we would sow and reap vegetables for our salads. We would stand up and walk to the TV to change the channel rather than reach for the remote control—or better yet, we would not watch TV at all. And our children, rather than playing on the computer, would play in the box that the computer came in!

But because this is not yet a perfect world, not all of us have the opportunity to become—and stay—In Sync. Children who are out of sync do not share the ease and comfort of an In-Sync child. These children may be clumsy, trip over themselves, avoid playground equipment, exhibit behavior problems, and have noticeably low self-esteem. They often develop into adults who are equally uncomfortable in their own bodies.

You may have a sense of when you are In Sync and when you are not. Have you ever noticed the correlation between moving and the way you feel? You may realize that when you are not In Sync, you can feel better simply by moving. When you come home exhausted after a long day of work and you go out to walk the dog around the block, or you drag yourself out to the gym, you feel better, right?

You feel better because you have moved!

Such movement is imperative to growing an In-Sync child. Because safe and purposeful movement experiences are not always readily available to the developing child, we offer this program to help you grow *your* In-Sync child. Our experience has taught us that an In-Sync child is a successful child.

This In-Sync Program will help your child *develop* the skills needed to check all the boxes in the list on page 3. If most of the boxes are already checked, use this program to *enhance* your child's skills. This program of enjoyable, easily incorporated activities will give your child a head start and a leg up.

It's About Time

▼

A S CHILD DEVELOPMENT specialists, we are delighted when we see children experiencing the world successfully. When we learn that children are struggling, we wonder, "Is it the *child* that is out of sync—or is it the *world*?"

These days, everyone seems to want to get things instantly—instant messaging, instant video games, instant credit, instant meals. We don't want to be kept waiting in traffic, on the telephone, or heaven forbid, by a trainee at the grocery store. It's as if we are shouting, "Quick! Now! No time to waste!"

Instant gratification may be possible when booting up a computer, but it is impossible when raising a child. Times may change, but the time required for a child to grow and develop never will. Human development permits no shortcuts.

We need to slow down and take our time. Allowing three minutes instead of ten seconds to get into a winter coat gives the developing child myriad opportunities for learning. And giving your toddler all the time she needs to go up and down the stairs is a gift.

Over the years, we have worked with thousands of children of all ages. We have also advised their parents and teachers in a variety of settings: individually and in groups, in the clinic and in the classroom, and as consultants and public speakers. Our combined seventy-plus years of work have made us aware that things are not the way they used to be. Our society has lost sight of the value of taking our time. We are concerned that children have neither the freedom nor the inclination to move and play the way they did years ago. This lack of movement is a major contributor to such problems as:

- Sensory processing disorder
- Visual processing difficulties
- Auditory processing difficulties, affecting speech and language
- Learning issues and academic difficulties
- Poor organization skills
- Inappropriate social skills
- Poor communication skills
- Self-esteem issues, resulting in an increase in childhood anxiety and teenage suicide
- Childhood obesity

The culprit is our out-of-sync culture, which no longer fosters physical activity. The balance has shifted toward emphasizing technology and academics at the expense of movement. In the past, children used their bodies to walk to school, do chores, help harvest and prepare food, and keep moving. They learned new skills when their bodies and brains were ready. Today, the emphasis on early academic achievements and technological expertise, as well as the modern conveniences all around us, have resulted in a world in which sedentary activities have become the norm. It is almost as if movement is no longer necessary. But movement *is* necessary, as we will see. . . .

THINK OUTSIDE the box; in fact, just think *outside*! Are flash cards and workbooks part of your child's routine? You can modify almost any written, academic chore into an enjoyable outdoor activity. Indeed, adding a movement component will enrich the learning experience. For example, if Bo is learning letters, have him try to form the letters with his whole body or jump on the shape of the humongous letter you have drawn with chalk on the sidewalk. If Lucia enjoys prewriting workbook activities, adapt the task from the page to your yard. Then, rather than moving her pencil to connect the dots, let her move her whole body by marching or rolling from spot to spot.

Movement Gets Us In Sync

▼

PEDIATRICIANS, TEACHERS, and other early childhood specialists now recognize that early motor development is one of the most important factors in the physical, emotional, academic, and overall success of your child.

In the past, as children walked and became more independent, they went outside to play. They climbed trees, jumped in puddles, played hopscotch, and rolled down hills. By doing so, their brains were learning all about the concepts of up and down, right and left, forward and back—many of the skills crucial for the acquisition of reading, writing, and being In Sync.

Think of the developing child as a tree. The stronger the roots, the more nutrients will be absorbed, the more anchored the tree will be, and the sturdier the trunk and branches will grow. A child with strong roots is likely to mature into a sturdy, thriving, blossoming individual.

How does the "In-Sync child" grow? We think of a child's roots as having three major components—sensory processing skills, perceptual motor skills, and visual skills. The In-Sync Program nourishes your child's roots by focusing on these components. These skills begin to develop before or soon after birth and are continuously integrated as the child moves.

Starting with *sensory processing*, let's see how little Tim, a typically developing baby, depends on these skills as he grows.

In the months before birth, Tim has countless movement adventures. These include every move his mother makes, his own flips and turns in the uterus, and his twisting journey through the birth canal. Each move counts toward strengthening the roots of the In-Sync child.

After birth, Tim busily takes in vast amounts of sensory information, the groundwork for all future learning. While all senses are operating, his tactile (touch), vestibular (movement and balance), and proprioceptive (position) senses are primary.

Tactile processing is receiving sensations through the skin and hair and then responding to those sensations. The tactile (or touch) sense is a primary source of information for the child about his connection to the world. The child whose brain accurately interprets tactile input is comfortable being touched by other people or objects. He uses his tactile sense to touch others appropriately and to learn about the texture, temperature, and shape of objects. He can discriminate one touch sensation from another—for example, wet from dry and hard from soft. Some daily life activities that require efficient tactile processing include:

- Wearing clothing of various textures
- Eating food of various textures
- Being physically close to other people
- Using scissors, pencils, forks, and spoons
- Sitting in a chair

Vestibular processing is taking in sensations about the pull of gravity through the inner ear and then responding to these sensations. This information tells the child about where her head is in relation to the surface of the earth—for example, whether she is upright, lying down, or about to fall when she leans too far back in her chair. The vestibular (or movement) sense is necessary to help her develop and coordinate the motions of her eyes, head, and body, so that she can develop good balance, muscle tone, vision, and hearing. Some daily life skills that require efficient vestibular processing include:

- Standing independently without leaning on another person or object
- Walking across an unstable surface, for example, gravel or an uneven sidewalk
- Riding a bicycle
- Riding in a car or elevator without motion sickness
- Sitting upright at a table or desk

WHEN JOHN NEEDS a dose of something and you don't know what, give him something to push, pull, lift, or carry. Each one of these vigorous actions develops and enhances his proprioception . . . and it feels good.

Proprioception is the unconscious awareness of sensations coming from muscles and joints. This information tells the child whether he is stomping or tiptoeing, how hard to press down on a pencil, and how to stretch his arm to pull out the seat belt. The proprioceptive (or position) sense helps the child know how to push his foot into his boot, lift his glass of milk without spilling, and bend his knees while jumping. Some other skills requiring efficient proprioception are:

- Climbing, running, crawling, rolling smoothly
- Biting off a mouthful of food and chewing it
- Cutting food with knife and fork
- Writing
- Manipulating small toys and delicate objects without breakage

As Tim moves through his first months of life, he begins to hold up his head, roll over, reach, and eventually move himself through space. While suckling and cuddling, he is taking in positive tactile input. Through his vestibular and proprioceptive senses, he receives information about his movements.

Tim begins to regulate his eye movements, too. With his budding visual sense, he can see motionless objects nearby, as well as people and things moving around him. He anticipates and imitates his parents' facial expressions.

Vestibular and proprioceptive sensations also affect his posture and muscle tone. He tries new movements and, after some effort, succeeds. To resist gravity, he lifts his head and shoulders, and arching up with his weight on his hands and abdomen, he twists from side to side and looks around.

Tim learns to respond to sounds. He hears a door shut and looks in the direction that the sound came from. He hears someone say his name and turns to greet the person. The more he moves, the more confident he becomes while exploring the world.

Meanwhile, as Tim moves, his *perceptual motor skills*, which depend upon a sound sensory processing base, begin to emerge and strengthen. These perceptual motor skills include balance, bilateral coordination, body awareness, directionality, laterality, midline crossing, motor planning, and spatial awareness.

Balance is defined in two ways. Static balance refers to being in place. It is what helps a child maintain a seated position or stand on one foot. Dynamic balance refers to moving. It is what helps a child hop across the room or walk across a balance beam. Balance begins to develop as the baby learns to hold up his head. A more refined level of balance is established as he learns to creep on hands and knees. Some other activities requiring good static and dynamic balance are:

- Riding a bike
- Standing on tiptoes
- Climbing stairs
- Skating
- Sitting in a chair

Bilateral coordination is the ability to move both sides of the body at the same time. An excited baby waves both arms simultaneously. As she matures, she will learn to move one side separately from the other. Bilateral coordination is especially important to support binocular vision, the ability to use both eyes as a team. Bilateral coordination permits the child to catch a beach ball, bat a baseball, and press Legos together. Some other activities requiring good bilateral coordination are:

- Clapping
- Holding a baby bottle
- Eating corn on the cob
- Pushing a stroller
- Swinging on a swing

WHEN OFFERING JAIMY both your hands, you are encouraging his bilateral coordination. Any time you encourage bilateral coordination, you are encouraging binocularity.

Body awareness is the mental picture of one's own body parts, where they are, how they interrelate, and how they move. Body awareness helps the child know where her hands, neck, ankles, and knees are. She can draw a relatively accurate self-portrait, with her body parts in the traditional places. She can orient her limbs to get dressed and change position to wriggle through a jungle gym. Some activities requiring good body awareness are:

■ Maneuvering through an obstacle course
■ Playing "Simon Says"
■ Getting into a car seat
■ Following directions
■ Interacting successfully with others

Directionality is the awareness of concepts such as up, down, forward, backward, sideways, and diagonally, and the ability to move in these directions on command. Directionality develops as the child actively moves himself through space. Directionality is particularly important as children learn to read and write. It allows them to see a "b" as a "b" and a "p" as a "p," not as a "d" or a "q." It helps them with math skills. For example, directionality makes it easy to walk backward, a skill children need to master subtraction. Some activities requiring good directionality are:

■ Reading maps
■ Cutting paper dolls
■ Parking the car
■ Negotiating through a crowded corridor
■ Tying shoes

Laterality is the awareness of the two sides of the body and the ability to move either side independently of the other. When playing the violin or patting your head and rubbing your tummy, laterality makes it possible for the left hand and the right hand to make two entirely different movements. Laterality begins to develop as the baby crawls and is further integrated as the child learns to walk and run. (Children who crawl briefly, or not at all, frequently have trouble with activities that require the awareness of sidedness, such as handwriting or reading.) Some other daily life activities that require laterality include:

- Brushing teeth
- Zipping and unzipping
- Cutting food
- Working a pencil sharpener
- Kicking a ball

JUST FOR FUN, ask Stephen to try using his nondominant hand to do everything that he usually does with his dominant hand. You should try it, too. Once in a while, hold the telephone or brush your teeth with your nondominant hand. Chew on the opposite side. Makes you aware of the importance of laterality, doesn't it? Isn't laterality cool?

Midline crossing is the ability to use a hand, foot, or eye across the invisible vertical line that runs down the center of the body. Midline crossing is especially important for integrating the two sides of the body as well as the two sides of the world. The ability to put together two sides makes it possible to develop good visual tracking, read and write, establish a hand preference, and play games such as patty cake. Some other daily life activities that require midline crossing include:

- Playing sports
- Kicking a ball
- Stirring pancake batter
- Dressing
- Parallel parking

Motor planning is the ability to organize and sequence the steps of an unfamiliar and complex body movement in a coordinated manner. A child develops motor planning by solving challenges with his body, such as climbing into his car seat, going down a slide, or dressing himself. This skill allows a child to maneuver through an obstacle course, master handwriting, and play sports. Some other activities that require motor planning include:

- Getting into a swing
- Getting in and out of a car
- Making a sandwich
- Putting on a jacket
- Typing on a keyboard

Spatial awareness is the understanding of space and where one is in relation to the surrounding world. Children become aware of spatial relationships by moving through space. A child who crawls across the room learns much more about spatial dimensions than one who is carried across the same space. Effective spatial awareness allows a child to maneuver around furniture, other people, and moving playground equipment; to do neat paperwork; and to organize his personal space, such as his bedroom, desk, and locker. Some other daily life activities that require spatial awareness include:

- Playing safely on a playground
- Bringing a forkful of food to one's mouth
- Tying shoes
- Doing puzzles
- Stacking blocks

What is Baby Tim up to now? He is developing body awareness, the mental picture of where his body parts are, how they interrelate, and how they move. Visual feedback adds to his body awareness. Along with body awareness comes bilateral (two-sided) coordination. This is the process that enables Tim to use both sides of his body symmetrically, in a simultaneous and coordinated way.

Tim begins to crawl on his tummy, then creep. Creeping on hands and knees is a crucial stage in the growing of an In-Sync child. Indeed, by creeping, Tim is developing and enhancing *all* the sensory, perceptual motor, and visual components of an In-Sync child. He gets vestibular input as he raises himself onto all fours, balances, and moves forward. He gets tactile and proprioceptive input every time he places his hands and knees on the ground. He develops laterality as he alternates his hands and knees, and because alternating body sides stimulates both sides of his brain, he strengthens his bilateral coordination. As laterality matures, Tim will become comfortable crossing his midline with his eyes, hands, and feet.

Another perceptual motor skill Tim learns while creeping is directionality as he makes decisions about where to go. Directionality will enable him to move his body for playground games, write with his pencil, and many years hence, drive a car from home to his girlfriend's house.

Creeping also promotes the all-important skill of motor planning. Motor planning allows Tim to do something he has never done before, and then do it again. Pulling himself up to a standing position, for example, requires motor planning the first few times, until he has practiced it so often that he can pull himself up effortlessly.

As Tim's sensory processing skills and perceptual motor skills take root, his *visual processing skills* grow, as well. Visual processing is the interpretation and response to information received through the eyes. Refined visual skills develop as Tim uses his eyes to function throughout his day. Reaching for his rattle, creeping across the floor, and running to his teacher all improve his vision. He looks where he is going and goes where he is looking. Indeed, the more he moves, the more his visual skills strengthen and mature.

Vision plays a very significant role, often unrecognized, in becoming and being In Sync. Early visual skills emerge from strong tactile, vestibular, and proprioceptive sensory systems and continue to develop simultaneously with perceptual motor skills—as long as Tim continues to move. Some essential visual processing skills are acuity, binocularity, and visual tracking.

Acuity is the measurement of sight, most often represented by the ratio 20/20, which is considered perfect eyesight. A baby, however, comes into the world with a visual acuity of 20/200! This means he can see 10 percent as well as a person with perfect acuity. As he matures and begins to take an interest in objects at a closer range, his acuity should naturally stabilize at 20/20. Acuity is a measurement of sight only, and should not be confused with vision, which is the interpretation of what one sees. Some daily life activities that require good acuity include:

- Recognizing letters and numbers
- Recognizing a friend's face
- Threading beads and lacing shoes
- Sorting buttons
- Discriminating the corn from the lima beans in the succotash

Binocularity is the ability to use both eyes together. This is crucial for depth perception. Any activity that encourages bilateral coordination also reinforces binocularity. You may see a child with poor binocularity lay his head on the desk or on his arm while reading or writing. When doing this, he is using only one eye to see. This habit should always be discouraged. Some daily life skills that require efficient binocularity include:

- Playing hopscotch
- Judging distances
- Running accurately toward a target
- Holding one's head straight rather than tilting it to one side
- Stepping onto an escalator

SIGHT VS. VISION

LOOK AT THE picture below. If you have not seen it before, you probably see shades of black, white, and gray in a nonsensical pattern. On the other hand, if you have seen this picture before, you know exactly what it is and recognize it immediately. Once you get it, you get it forever.

(Holy cow! Still can't see it? Answer is on page 21.)

How does this happen?

At first glance, your brain does not know what to do with such a confusing picture. Because you have seen nothing quite like it, you cannot associate or compare it with anything else. You do not have a visual "hook" for it. If you have adequate eyesight, you can *see* it, of course. But you cannot interpret it unless, over time, you have developed the necessary visual skills to *process* it. Vision allows you to process and thus to make sense of what you see.

Efficient visual processing requires many skills. To make sense of the whole picture, your brain uses acuity, tracking, binocularity, and other visual skills to process what the eyes see. A growing child requires months and years of visual experiences to develop these skills. Moving through space—playing Hide-and-Seek, hiking up a hill, swinging—develops and enhances visual skills. These skills do not, cannot, and will not develop smoothly if children glue their eyes to an electronic screen for hours each day.

Visual tracking is the ability to watch a moving target using only the eyes, with no head movement. Visual tracking develops as the infant begins to watch moving things such as a mobile or a parent. A child with poor visual tracking may frequently lose her place while reading, may reverse words, and may have midline crossing issues as the eyes fail to move smoothly from left to right (or right to left). Some daily life skills that require efficient visual tracking include:

- Reading a sentence in a book
- Reading from the chalkboard
- Reading sheet music
- Playing ball sports
- Avoiding getting hit by a moving swing or car

WHEN HANDING SOMETHING to Sandra, or when taking something from her, always be sure that she *looks* at your hand. Encouraging her to *look* at what she is doing teaches her to use her eyes to direct her movements, while simultaneously improving her tracking skills. When you hand Sandra a toy, don't just put it in her hand. Rather, move the toy here and there a couple of times until she looks at what she is taking. When she gives you a toy, don't just take it from her; rather, move your hand here and there to make her *look* at the toy's destination. Make it fun!

As Tim evolves into a walker, getting to his feet and learning to walk and run, his vision becomes more precise. He can interpret visual data more accurately. He understands spatial relationships and can discriminate where people and objects are and where he is in relation to them.

Tim can hold a crayon, draw a simple picture, catch a ball, and pour juice. Soon his developing sensory, perceptual motor, and visual processing will ready Tim to ride his tricycle through a simple maze and eventually play T-ball or trumpet, whichever he chooses.

THREE "IN-SYNC" COMPONENTS

TRY BALANCING ON one foot while focusing on a target. Now close your eyes. Does your balance change? Of course! You may feel shaky, or you may lose your balance altogether. This is a perfect example of the interrelationship of the In-Sync components: sensory, perceptual motor, and visual.

(The picture on page 19 is a cow, looking right at you!)

Being In Sync

▼

N OW THAT YOU understand the In-Sync components and their interrelationship in Tim's early development, take a look at how fundamental they are for functioning in the adult world. Just consider the first ten minutes of a typical day . . .

Responding to the Alarm Clock
- Roll over to look at the clock *(vestibular processing, directionality, motor planning, visual processing)*.
- Reach for the alarm clock *(proprioception)*.
- Press the button *(proprioception, tactile processing, laterality)*.

Getting Out of Bed
- Sit up *(proprioception, vestibular processing, balance, motor planning)*.
- Put your feet on the floor *(tactile processing, bilateral coordination, motor planning)*.
- Stand up *(proprioception, vestibular processing, balance, motor planning)*.

Heading to the Bathroom

- Walk through the door *(proprioception, vestibular processing, balance, directionality, laterality, spatial awareness, motor planning, visual processing)*.
- Use the toilet.
  - Optional: Raise the lid *(proprioception, tactile processing, laterality)*.
  - Sit or stand *(proprioception, vestibular processing, body awareness, balance, motor planning)*.
  - Flush the toilet *(proprioception)*.
- Use the sink.
  - Get there *(proprioception, vestibular processing, balance, directionality, laterality, spatial awareness, motor planning)*.
  - Turn on the faucet(s) *(proprioception, tactile processing, directionality, bilateral coordination or laterality)*.
  - Wash hands *(tactile processing, body awareness, bilateral coordination, vestibular processing, balance)*.
- Brush your teeth.
  - Reach for the toothbrush and toothpaste *(proprioception, tactile processing, laterality, spatial awareness, visual processing)*.
  - Unscrew the toothpaste cap and place toothpaste on the toothbrush *(proprioception, tactile processing, laterality)*.
  - Brush the teeth *(proprioception, tactile processing, body awareness, laterality, directionality, midline crossing, motor planning)*.

. . . and this is just the first ten minutes of your day! Think of how many skills are necessary for each task just to get you up and through your bathroom routine. Now multiply that number times all the minutes in an hour and all the hours in your day. Everything you do requires the successful integration of many, many skills and abilities.

In your child's life, a task such as writing or catching a ball requires the same integration of skills and abilities. When these tasks do not come easily, we sometimes neglect to uncover the underlying reasons. Trying to help, we frequently use the wrong approach.

Let's look at the skill of writing one's name. Many children are encouraged to practice writing their names before they are developmentally ready to do so. Practice does not always make perfect! Every parent and teacher should realize that before the child is expected to write, he should be able to master many earlier skills first.

A child who is taught to form his letters before he is ready will frequently run into difficulty later on when he is expected to write for content. As you look at the chart below, consider whether your child is really ready to write his name easily—or needs more time to move his entire body.

PREREQUISITES TO WRITING

Before a Child Can . . .	He Needs . . .	Which He Developed by . . .
Sit upright in chair, hold body and head still when writing	Balance	• Holding head up when lying on stomach • Creeping on all fours • Walking without support • Stopping easily when running
Hold pencil in hand	Tactile processing	• Feeding self Cheerios • Playing with Duplos, Legos • Painting and/or scribbling with crayon • Stringing beads
Hold paper still with one hand while other hand moves pencil	Laterality	• Creeping on all fours • Climbing stairs, alternating feet • Being proficient at one-handed tasks (painting at an easel, throwing a ball) • Establishing a preferred hand

Before a Child Can . . .	He Needs . . .	Which He Developed by . . .
Recognize circles and lines in letters	Directionality	• Moving in various directions when asked • Imitating another person's movements, especially of arms • Reproducing patterns with parquetry blocks • Playing successfully with jigsaw puzzles
Use blank area of paper effectively	Spatial awareness	• Maneuvering easily through obstacle courses • Enjoying playground equipment • Pouring juice • Knowing where he is in space
Write smoothly across the page	Midline crossing	• Reproducing an "X" on paper • Reaching across his midline rather than changing hands • Watching moving target without head movement • Touching hands to opposite knees
See what he is doing	Visual processing	• Having adequate visual acuity to work at a desk • Making and holding eye contact • Playing matching games • Recognizing shapes and letters
Know how to make his hand and arm move as he wants them to	Motor planning	• Getting dressed • Getting in and out of his car seat • Using utensils to eat • Moving fluidly with purpose

As you can see, writing does not just happen. It takes years to develop the underlying skills for this complex task—years of moving to prepare the child to sit quietly at a desk.

Now let's look at the skill of catching a ball. A similar developmental sequence is necessary. Whereas handwriting is taught in school, catching a ball is a skill that often happens naturally.

What happens when catching a ball does not happen naturally? The child may choose not to play ball, because it is frustrating and unsatisfying.

So, does going out in the backyard and tossing a ball help? While this activity can be a great bonding experience, it can also be a negative experience if your child is not ready. Thus, before grabbing a football and stepping outside, study the chart below to gauge whether or not your child is In Sync for the game that you have in mind.

PREREQUISITES TO CATCHING A BALL

Before a Child Can . . .	She Needs . . .	Which She Developed by . . .
Stand independently	Balance	• Holding head up when lying on stomach • Creeping on all fours • Walking without support • Stopping easily when running
Use hands together	Bilateral coordination	• Waving both hands at crib mobile • Pressing both hands on floor to raise upper body • Holding bottle with both hands to feed herself • Holding large beach ball
Watch a moving target	Visual tracking	• Gazing at a crib mobile • Watching a parent approach across the room • Watching a toy train • Chasing a ball
Position self to catch a ball	Motor planning	• Turning over in crib • Orienting limbs for dressing • Climbing into car seat • Maneuvering through obstacle course

Three Children Get In Sync

▼

MAGINE WHAT IT is like for children who are expected to do more than their bodies are ready to do. Any one of the In-Sync components that your child has not yet fully integrated can significantly compromise his or her ability to succeed in the world.

We recall three children whose difficulties illustrate the importance of establishing a firm foundation. These children required early intervention. (Of course, most children develop just fine, especially when movement is incorporated into everything they do.)

FROM SHRINKING VIOLET TO BLOSSOMING ROSE

Rosie comes to Kids Moving Company when she has just turned six. She gives the impression of being small because of the way she holds herself, contracting inward. On the playground, she shrinks from group play. Her movements are tentative. Her voice is very soft.

At the dinner table, Rosie props up her head with her hand. At school, she rests her head on her desk. Both at home and at school, she is very cooperative, but her teachers sometimes wish she would be more assertive.

Rosie's pediatrician suggests that she may need psychotherapy, as her self-esteem appears to be very low. Because Rosie's parents jog and play tennis regularly, they are aware of the role that movement plays in feeling good. They decide to offer their daughter a moving experience before following through on the pediatrician's suggestion.

At their first meeting, Joye offers Rosie several movement challenges, including moving through an obstacle course, jumping across the room, and catching and bouncing a ball. She notices that Rosie is fatiguing rapidly, and they move to the table, where Joye shows Rosie the following shapes, one at a time.

As she shows each shape, she asks Rosie to copy it on a sheet of paper. Here is what Rosie's paper looks like:

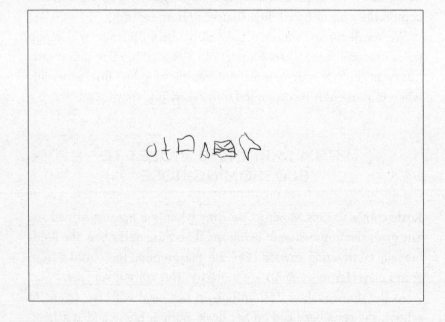

Notice how Rosie draws all the shapes in miniature and crams them all into the center of her paper. The lines in her divided rectangle (the fifth shape) fail to cross at the center, suggesting a lack of midline crossing. Her spacing on the paper tells us, above all, that Rosie does not have good spatial awareness, which is the understanding of space and where one is in relation to the surrounding world. Rosie's placement of the shapes in relation to the paper could be a reflection of the way she perceives herself in relation to the environment around her.

Because spatial awareness develops as the child rolls, creeps, toddles, and eventually runs through the world, logically the way to promote spatial skills is by rolling, creeping, toddling, and running. These movement activities will also address Rosie's underlying difficulties with proprioceptive and vestibular processing, suggested by her poor posture. Sitting at a table with a pencil or in front of a computer with a mouse will do her no good.

Joye could choose to have Rosie repeatedly practice drawing the shapes, even directing her where to place them on the paper. After many practice sessions, Rosie's paper would probably look perfect—but this tedious repetition of a single task would not solve the underlying problem.

Instead, Joye and Rosie play movement games that encourage Rosie to move her *whole body* through space. The goal of the therapy is to expand her world. Over the next few months, Rosie does In-Sync activities, such as Arm Circles (page 97), Balloon Buffoon (page 62), Bye, Bye Bubbles (page 66), How Many Steps? (page 174), and Rolling Log (page 144). As her sensory processing improves, she is better able to move her body and thus to understand where she is in space.

After a few months of playful work together, Joye reintroduces the shapes and asks Rosie to copy them. This is how her second paper looks:

As you can see, Rosie's second paper shows a much better organization of space. The vertical, horizontal, and diagonal lines in her divided rectangle intersect accurately, indicating a maturing grasp of spatial relationships. And because her therapy was movement-based, her newfound sense of organization is also obvious in the way Rosie holds herself, her exuberant participation on the playground, and her comfort mingling with her peers.

FROM BULLY TO BUDDY

Bernie's sixth grade teacher has concerns about his aggressive behavior, poor math grades, and difficulty with reading and writing. Bernie has worked with a tutor twice a week for the past month, but his teacher and worried parents have seen no improvement. His parents bring him to Kids Moving Company at his pediatrician's suggestion.

Joye learns from his parents that Bernie never crawled and was an early walker. He never sits still. He is, in their words, "all over the place." His bedroom is a disaster area, as are his three-ring binder, school locker, and desk.

Bernie does not excel at soccer, even though his parents describe his gross motor skills as "excellent." He is rarely chosen for a team because he wants to make, but not follow, the rules.

During his first visit to Kids Moving Company, Joye watches Bernie attempt various motor tasks and sees that although he succeeds, he does so with great difficulty. Joye notices how hard he must concentrate on tasks that should be simple, such as marching in a pattern. She notices his clenched fists when he jumps on two feet or skips. This tells us that Bernie struggles mightily to move his body effectively. When that's the case, how can a boy be comfortable in his body—and in the big world?

More evidence of Bernie's internal disorganization is his representation of the same shapes that Rosie copied. Here is Bernie's paper:

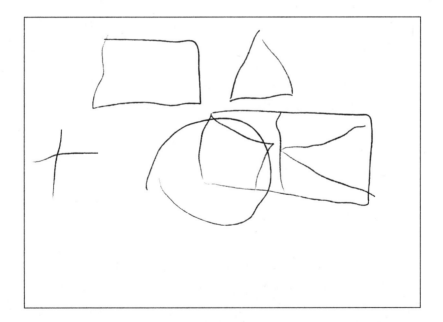

Notice how Bernie draws his divided rectangle on top of his circle. He shows no organization in his work. Like Rosie's paper, Bernie's paper shows us that he, too, has poor spatial awareness. This is not surprising, as he never crawled, and because he never crawled, his laterality and midline crossing are also likely to be poorly developed.

Whereas a goal of Rosie's program is to open her up, a goal of Bernie's program is to rein him in. In his case, as in hers, working at a desk is not going to be helpful. Bernie needs to move through the early developmental steps that he missed. He begins on the ground with In-Sync activities such as Nose to Knee (page 134), Roll-a-Path (page 180), Scootie Cutie (page 86), Watch Your Hands Creep (page 164), and Wheelbarrow (page 90). These activities will give Bernie the fundamental skills he missed by walking before he was really ready. Once the roots are established, Bernie will use his body more effectively and efficiently as he moves purposefully through space.

Look at Bernie's second paper after four months of In-Sync activities:

Notice how his accuracy and organization have improved. Now he is beginning to understand math skills because he is beginning to internalize concepts of left and right (laterality and midline crossing) and up and down (directionality).

Furthermore, through the activities that encouraged Bernie to use his body in new ways, his motor planning shows dramatic improvement. He now easily finds his homework in his binder, his long-lost sneakers under his bed, and himself in the middle of a winning team.

FROM CLUELESS TO COMPETENT

George, a member of the Teddy Bear class at St. Columba's Nursery School, is about to turn four, but his behavior is that of a younger child. In social interactions, where his peers "use their words," George uses his hands. At the table, while his classmates are constructing towers and houses with Legos, George purposelessly gathers and scatters the blocks. Walking down the hall, George drags his hand along the wall.

On the playground, he sits in one spot in the sandbox or leans against the teacher's leg. He refuses to get on the swing or the slide.

He takes a slap dash approach to art. At the easel, he smears a horizon across the paper without even looking at what his paintbrush is doing. Back at the table, he rushes through art projects with a minimum of interest.

George's teachers are confused because he is a sweet boy, yet he frequently ends up in a tussle with his classmates. His parents are concerned because no one wants to play with him.

Despite "normal" results from routine eyesight and sensory processing screenings, George's classroom teachers are still concerned. They share their observations with Carol, who has been teaching and consulting at St. Columba's for many years. She agrees that something may be going on and knows that the screenings were just screenings and therefore too cursory to pinpoint George's difficulty.

Carol suggests that some of his behaviors can be explained by poor visual processing. If George's visual system is not operating optimally, he may not understand where he is in space or how near or far he is to an object. Without consistent visual information to rely on, George may need to use his hands to "see," to balance, and to move.

So, Carol and Joye design a program of In-Sync activities for the teachers to integrate into their classroom and for George's parents to implement at home. The activities include Amazing Delivery Kid (page 61), Angel Wings (page 95), Car Seat Scramble (page 68), Eye Spy (page 112), Follow the Feather (page 119), and Hug Roll (page 76). Carol and Joye choose these activities in order to help George develop and enhance his visual processing, including binocularity for depth perception and tracking. Because an efficient visual system depends on an In-Sync body, these activities also address bilateral coordination and motor planning.

Fortunately, George's teachers understand that these activities benefit all the children in the Teddy Bear class, and so they incorporate one or more activities into the daily schedule. At home, George's parents embrace the program and are pleasantly surprised to see how quickly the activities become second nature.

Before long, George becomes an active participant on the playground, in the classroom, and at home. He takes pride in his Lego constructions and art projects. He begins to request playdates and becomes much more competent and independent.

Although Rosie, Bernie, and George are different ages and appear to have different needs, they all benefit greatly from the In-Sync Program. The reason is that In-Sync activities provide movement experiences that all children require to build a sturdy foundation. For various reasons, these three children were not comfortable using their bodies to move and therefore lost opportunities to grow optimally in their physical, social, and emotional development.

They are among the many kids we have treated or taught since our careers began in the 1970s. Their difficulties are representative of a myriad of behaviors that are often misunderstood, overlooked, misdiagnosed, or improperly treated. Using the In-Sync Program will help you to understand your child's sensory, perceptual motor, and visual processing development and to recognize a problem that may require professional intervention.

Of course, when your child is In Sync, these activities will further strengthen her developing skills and add to her delight in moving.

Each child's success excites us, and we want to share our enthusiasm with you. This easy program will quickly become invaluable to you, too, as you and your child learn to incorporate the concepts into your everyday lifestyle.

Tips on Growing an In-Sync Child

▼

❑ **Most kids develop in the same sequence, but not at the same rate.**

> Say this to yourself every day as you watch your child's development unfold. This is the basis of the In-Sync Program.

❑ **Childhood is a journey, not a race.**

> Sooner does not mean better. Always remember that motor development is sequential. Teaching a child a skill before he is ready to develop it *on his own* is not usually in the child's best interest. An out-of-sequence mastery is sometimes referred to as a "splinter skill." Often, parents misinterpret a child's desire to walk. Believing they are doing something in their child's best interest, they grasp their child's hands to move him along. But parents, please beware. This is not helpful and, in some cases, can be detrimental.

❑ **Slow is usually better than fast.**

> Quicker does not mean better. Almost all motor skills are more difficult *and* more beneficial when the child

practices them slowly. Practice of a basic skill makes subsequent skills easier to acquire. Left to their own devices, most children will know when it's time to move along to the next level. So, let your child linger at the level she's at, even if she lingers longer than you think is necessary. Let the baby crawl as long as she wants; she will walk *when she is ready*. Let her scramble in and out, in and out, in and out of the sandbox. What may look like unnecessary repetition to you is skill building to the child. There's no hurry.

❑ **Having fun helps kids succeed.**
We designed this program to be fun and functional— not only for your child but for you as well. So think of these activities as play, and don't worry about whether your child is learning anything. We promise you, he is!

You Are Already Growing an In-Sync Child

▼

E VERY TIME YOU . . .

- Bounce your child on your knee
- Let your child walk in your shoes
- Put your child on the carpet and then the bedspread and then the grass
- Let your child roll down a hill
- Roll a ball to your child
- Toss a ball to your child
- Let your child get in and out of his car seat and stroller
- Let your child push his stroller and pull his wagon
- Let your child jump off the couch into a mound of pillows
- Let your child make her own bed
- Let your child bang on the floor with a wooden spoon
- Let your child feed himself and smear his face with food
- Let your child jump in a puddle
- Give your child a sponge in the bathtub
- Roughhouse with your child
- Hug your child tightly

. . . you help your child take another step along the In-Sync continuum.

PART TWO

Getting Started with the In-Sync Program

About the In-Sync Program

▼

T HE IN-SYNC PROGRAM is designed to give your child the movement experiences he needs to get In Sync. As opposed to computer and video programs and other sedentary activities, the In-Sync Program requires your child to move, because we know that fundamental skills are acquired only by moving. No time spent passively in front of a screen can teach your child what actively moving can.

What makes the In-Sync Program unique?

Each In-Sync activity is . . .

- **Developmentally based.** The activities are organized into three levels:
  - Beginner—skills of a typical preschooler
  - Intermediate—skills of a typical primary school child
  - Advanced—skills of a typical elementary school child
  - In addition, all activities include suggestions for more challenging moves as kids develop more skills.

- **Flexible and adaptable.** Each activity includes ways to customize the movement experiences to suit your child's specific needs. Because your child is unique, because your child is better at some moves than others, because your child has definite preferences, and because nobody enjoys the same old exercises day after day, please feel free to get creative! Sometimes simply changing instructions from "fast" to "slow" or from "way up high" to "way down low" can make a familiar activity seem brand-new.
- **Addressing many skills simultaneously.** Rather than concentrating on one skill at a time, these activities incorporate many basic sensory, motor, and visual skills. The primary skills addressed are listed near the beginning of each activity.

The In-Sync Program is . . .
- **Easy to use.** With easy-to-follow instructions and minimal equipment, you can begin the program today.
- **Portable.** Take this program anywhere and everywhere, from your living room to the playground to the checkout line in the grocery store.
- **Expandable.** With the activities in this book and the variations you and your child are sure to invent, the number of In-Sync experiences is infinite.
- **Inclusive.** Once you are comfortable with the In-Sync Program, you will see how easy it becomes to include siblings and friends. Indeed, encourage everyone to join the activities, which put the "fun" back into "functional"!
- **Economical.** The only monetary investment is the cost of this book, other than some simple and optional equipment. The big investment is not your dollars, but your time—and the payoff is priceless.

In just a few minutes a day, you will be giving your child a moving experience that will last a lifetime.

Choosing an In-Sync Activity

▼

S O, HOW DO you get started? Here are four ways:

1. Determine where your child's skill level lies on the continuum from Beginner to Advanced. Remember, these levels are flexible and merely guidelines. Then glance at the table of contents and choose an activity that appeals to you, or . . .
2. In the appendix, look at the Index of In-Sync Activities, where the activities are grouped into various categories such as, "Good for Visual Processing," or "Good for When You Have No Equipment," or . . .
3. Take a look at the sample menus below, or . . .
4. Just dig in! If the activity you choose is too easy, we offer ways to make it more challenging. If it is too hard, choose another one.

Our hope is that you will quickly customize the program to suit you and your child's needs by integrating your own personal touches.

SAMPLE MENUS FOR THE IN-SYNC PROGRAM

Five In-Sync Activities For . . .

When Your Child Is Out of Sorts

Can't Tap Me—to engage your child and bring him close

Arm Circles—to get him moving

Flashlight Tag—to help him focus

Angel Wings—to calm him

Hug Roll—to provide proprioception, deep pressure, and love

Instead of Going to the Playground

Scootie Cutie—to get your child moving

Ball Bounce—to help her focus

Roll-a-Path—to move her whole body through space

Wheelbarrow—to provide proprioception

Pillow Pile—to provide vigorous movement without getting dirty

A Trip to the Grocery Store

Car Seat Scramble—to help your child get moving

How Many Steps?—to engage his vision and get him thinking

Eye Spy—to make finding an item fun

Can't Tap Me—to keep him engaged

Amazing Delivery Kid—to provide proprioception and get your groceries in the door

Preparing to Do Homework

Gopher—to arouse your child and ready her for thinking

Wake Up, Arms!—to prepare her for handwriting

Make-a-Ball—to improve her hand and finger dexterity

Tap Me Silly—to get her hands and eyes moving together

Hip, Hip Hooray!—to organize her whole body for getting an A+

Instead of Video Games

Write Through Me—to improve your child's mental imagery

Watch Your Hands Creep—to help him focus

Penny Pass—to improve visual tracking

Flashlight Focus—to improve eye-hand-foot coordination

Pipe Cleaner Poke—to improve accuracy to get to the next level

Just Because

Angel Wings—to warm up your child's body

Rolling Log—to jump-start his sensory systems

Wheelbarrow—to develop his upper body strength

Watch Your Hands Creep—to engage his visual system and improve his laterality

Tap Me Silly—to improve midline crossing while laughing

Before Bedtime

Look Ma, No Hands!—to get your child down the hall to the bathroom

Red Cup, Blue Cup—to make her bath time fun and productive

Reach for the Sky—to help her get into her pajamas

Hug Roll—to ready her for sweet dreams

Good Night, Flashlight—to wish her good night

A Child with an Affinity for Music (one a day, because these activities take longer than others)

Drumroll, Please

Heads Up, Toes Down

Keyboard Tales

Shape Rain

Singing String

We encourage you to create your own categories and menus. You might enjoy updating and referring to them over time.

Guidelines for Using the In-Sync Program

▼

WHILE WORKING TO help your child along his natural progression of skill acquisition, keep in mind several important guidelines:

1. Be sure that your child fully understands the directions involved in the activity you are asking him to do.
2. Restrain yourself from being overprotective and overhelpful, and be sure that the environment is safe and comfortable. A child needs a certain degree of independence in order to realize his own potential.
3. Give your child an opportunity to practice the activity and be sure that the experience is gratifying and fun. If he is unsuccessful, have him practice a skill he has already mastered. Remember that success is a powerful motivator. If he feels that he is successful, he will want to do more and more. If he feels he is unsuccessful at an activity that he is not ready for, he will be discouraged from trying again and may delay the emergence of the correct pattern.

4. Remember that when a child first discovers a new motor skill, it may appear clumsy and awkward; after practice, it will become more refined. Encourage your child's achievement, no matter how awkward the attempt may appear to you.

5. Repeat favorite activities from time to time. Once your child has mastered the activity, she may still enjoy doing it, and it will certainly continue to enhance her development. Repetition is a wonderful tool for learning.

Have fun!

Instead of This. . .	Say This
Do it this way.	Show me your way to do this.
Your body is not straight.	Is your body in a straight line?
Hurry up.	Can you do it more slowly?
You are not finished yet.	Let's do it one more time.
You have to . . .	Have you . . . ?
It is not that hard.	Of course, it is hard. You can do it.
Why can't you do this yet?	You are getting the hang of it.
No, that is not right.	I love the way you tried . . .
What, you are already tired?	Let's take a break.
That was not so bad, was it?	Wow, was that ever fun!
No, that is not what the book says.	What a great idea!

Checklists for the In-Sync Program

▼

BEFORE GETTING STARTED, please refer to the following checklists.

Before Starting an In-Sync Activity

- ❑ Have you read the book up to this point, and are you comfortable with the concepts presented?
- ❑ Have you read through the directions to the activity so that you clearly understand them?
- ❑ Is the space you are using ample and safe? If the activity requires your child to roll across the floor, is the space obstacle-free and large enough for him to roll several times? If the activity requires your child to move her arms to her sides and in front of her, can she do it without knocking over lamps?
- ❑ Do you have the materials you need?
- ❑ Do you have a pen or pencil ready to jot down notes?
- ❑ Are you ready to have fun?

Week 1 Checklist

During the In-Sync activity

❑ Does your child understand the directions?

❑ Are you enthusiastic and supportive in body language and tone of voice?

❑ If your child becomes frustrated, do you acknowledge it? Do you modify the activity or perhaps choose another?

❑ Are you and your child having fun?

After the activity

❑ Were you relaxed?

❑ Were the activities you chose appropriate for your child? Was your child engaged and challenged?

❑ Did you and your child have fun?

Week 2 Checklist

"Week 2" does not have to mean the second week. You will get to Week 2 when you can confidently check all the boxes in the Week 1 checklist. Remember, slow is often better than fast.

During the In-Sync activity

❑ Same as Week 1, *and . . .*

❑ Do you vary the instructions—*quickly, lightly, way up high, quietly*—that you give?

❑ Do you use prepositions—*beside, above, through, next to*—to change the activity slightly?

After the activity

❑ Same as Week 1, *and . . .*

❑ Are you building up a repertoire of favorites? Are you repeating some activities from the first week while adding new ones?

❑ Are you experimenting with the activities to make them your own?

❑ Are you and your child having fun?

Week 3 Checklist

During the In-Sync activity

❑ Same as Weeks 1 and 2, *and* . . .
❑ Are you introducing the "Ways to Make It More Challenging" techniques?
❑ Are you noticing improvement in your child's performance?

After the activity

❑ Same as Weeks 1 and 2, *and* . . .
❑ Can you do some activities without referring to this book?
❑ Are you and your child coming up with ideas for new activities?

Moving Forward

During the In-Sync activity

❑ Same as Weeks 1, 2, and 3, *and* . . .
❑ Are you integrating some of the In-Sync Program concepts into your family's day?
❑ Are you noticing positive changes in your child's:
    ❑ Motor skills?
    ❑ Mood?
    ❑ Stamina?
    ❑ Attention?
    ❑ Independence?
    ❑ Curiosity about the surrounding world?

PART THREE

The In-Sync Activities

Beginner Activities

AMAZING DELIVERY KID

Making kids feel needed is important. Even a toddler can carry a box of rice into the house. Naturally, this kind of help will slow down your routine; consider the time well spent.

Helps Your Child Develop and Enhance . . .
- Proprioception (for pushing, pulling, lifting, and carrying)
- Bilateral coordination (for playing with toys and using tools)
- Motor planning (for doing daily chores efficiently)

What You Need
- Bags of unbreakable groceries
- Unbagged groceries, such as a cantaloupe, a six-pack of juice boxes, or a sack of potatoes

What You Do
1. Say, "Danny, I need your help. Let's carry the groceries into the house together." Give Danny a range of bags and other items from which to choose.
2. Next time, ask him to carry two bags of groceries, one in each hand.
3. Let Danny experiment carrying in different weights, sizes, and shapes of groceries.

Ways to Make It More Challenging
- Vary Danny's path as he brings in the bags.
- Have him walk very slowly or sideways.
- Ask him to help sort the groceries and put them away.

What to Look For
- Danny is able to carry the load from car to kitchen.
- Danny can adjust his body to the weight of the bags.

BALLOON BUFFOON

This activity is fun for one and hilarious for two. The game inspires kids to come up with imaginative ways to transport a balloon across the room.

Helps Your Child Develop and Enhance . . .
- Bilateral coordination (for carrying a cafeteria tray and tying shoelaces)
- Body awareness (for bathing and grooming)
- Directionality (for moving in the correct direction)
- Motor planning (for figuring out how to stop and go)
- Proprioception (for digging and raking)
- Spatial awareness (for knowing how to space one's letters on the page)

What You Need
- Balloon
- Space to move
- Visual target

What You Do
1. Point out the visual target, such as a tree, a parked car, the front door, or a picture on the wall.
2. Give Holly an inflated balloon and let her toss and catch it and otherwise experiment with it.
3. Say, "Hold the balloon between your hands and walk toward the target."
4. Say, "Hold the balloon with your elbows and move toward the target."
5. Say, "Hold the balloon between your knees and jump toward the target."

Ways to Make It More Challenging

- Vary the way in which Holly moves toward the target:
  - Jumping
  - Galloping
  - Quietly
  - Slowly and way up high
- Vary the body parts Holly uses to hold the balloon, such as:
  - Same-side elbow and knee
  - Opposite elbow and knee
  - Ankles
  - Arm and torso
- Have Holly recite the alphabet or spell her name with each step, jump, etc.
- Challenge her and a friend to move around the space holding one balloon between various body parts, including:
  - Backs
  - Foreheads
  - Noses
  - Elbows
  - Different body parts from each other

What to Look For

- Holly holds the balloon with the body parts as requested.
- She can hold the balloon and look at the target while moving.
- When jumping, Holly is able to land on her two feet at the same time.

BOUNCING BABY

This game is popular and familiar. Around the world and since time began, grown-ups have bounced babies on their knees, with good reason. This simple activity answers the need everyone has to move rhythmically, to take in sensations of touch and movement, and to share a moment of fun.

Helps Your Child Develop and Enhance . . .
- Balance (for walking and running)
- Bilateral coordination (for doing push-ups and jumping jacks)
- Vestibular processing (for swaying in a hammock and swinging at the playground)

What You Need
- Bouncy ball, large enough to reach his knees if he were standing

What You Do
1. Place Herman on his tummy on the ball. Place your hand on his back and gently bounce him on the ball.
2. Keeping your hand on his back, carefully roll the ball from side to side, and forward and back.
3. Sit on the floor in front of Herman. Say, "Look at me." Hold Herman's hands and slowly roll him forward and back.
4. Seat Herman on the ball, holding him if necessary, and bounce him some more.

Ways to Make It More Challenging

- Hold both of Herman's hands in one of yours. Roll him around on the ball.
- Hold his feet while you gently roll him.
- Hold his hands, keeping your arms loose so that he has to generate movement all by himself.

What to Look For

- Herman enjoys being in the prone position.
- When seated, he strives to maintain his balance on the ball.

BYE, BYE BUBBLES

Catching, clapping, squeezing, and popping bubbles encourage many important perceptual motor skills. Playing with bubbles is always wonderful outdoors; playing with bubbles indoors works, too, in a space where it's all right to get a little messy.

Helps Your Child Develop and Enhance . . .

- Balance (for bike riding and stopping quickly when running)
- Bilateral coordination (for knitting and playing the piano)
- Laterality (for putting on gloves and socks)
- Midline crossing (for letter recognition and reading)
- Tactile processing (for peeling an orange and playing in the sand)
- Visual tracking (for doing mazes and reading maps)

What You Need

- Bubbles
- Telephone book
- Paper towel tube
- Optional: toothpicks

What You Do

1. Blow bubbles and ask Miri to catch them, any way she chooses. Try to blow only one or two bubbles at a time to make them easier to catch.
2. Ask Miri to stand on a telephone book to catch the bubbles.
3. Say:
   - "Clap a bubble between your hands. Just one at a time!"
   - "Squeeze one bubble at a time with one hand."
   - "Catch one bubble at a time, first with your right hand and then with your left hand."
4. Hold the paper towel roll vertically with both hands. Hand it to her and say, "Hold the paper towel roll this way with both hands. Try to catch a bubble on the top of the tube."

Ways to Make It More Challenging

- Miri pops each bubble with toothpicks held in each hand, first using both hands working toward the middle on each bubble, and then using one hand at a time.
- She stands on one foot.

What to Look For

- Miri *watches* the bubbles so she catches what she's looking at, rather than "catching" whatever happens to float in front of her.
- She keeps her feet in a stationary position.
- She uses both hands when asked to, and either hand separately when so instructed.
- She accurately alternates hands when she is instructed to.
- She keeps *both* hands on the paper towel tube at all times to ensure that she crosses the midline.

CAR SEAT SCRAMBLE

"I did it all by myself!" is a triumphant cry we love to hear from our toddlers. Regrettably, when we routinely complete everyday tasks for our children, they often miss out on the chance to develop essential skills. Although letting children crawl into their car seats may add a few extra minutes to your daily routine, it is a skill your child needs to master.

Helps Your Child Develop and Enhance . . .
- Motor planning (for pouring from the juice pitcher)
- Proprioception (for reaching for the juice pitcher)
- Spatial awareness (for putting the juice pitcher back where it was)

What You Need
- Car seat
- Bit of extra time and patience

What You Do
1. Set the car seat on the living room floor and hold the seat steady. Say, "Larry, into your seat you go!"
2. Let Larry figure out how to climb in all by himself.
3. Let Larry experiment with the buckles. When he is able to buckle himself in, encourage him to do so.

Ways to Make It More Challenging
- When the car seat is strapped into your car, alter the path that Larry needs to take to get to his seat: first, place Larry near the car seat; next, let him crawl over the front seat to get there.
- Alternate the placement of the car seat in the car—left side, middle, or right side.

What to Look For

- Larry appropriately uses his arms to pull himself and his legs to push himself.
- He figures out how to turn himself around so that he is facing the appropriate direction in his seat.
- Larry is buckled in safely!

CHANGE THE PLACEMENT of Nili's car seat, as often as possible, to encourage her to change how she looks at the world. Change the position of her bed pillow so that one week her head is at one end of the bed, and the next week, her head is at the other end. This will allow Nili to view the world from a different vantage point from the one she is used to.

FLASHLIGHT TAG

Turn off the lights, switch on a flashlight, and get ready for gales of giggles. This enormously entertaining flashlight activity is high energy, while its counterpart, Good Night, Flashlight (page 72), is calming. (We recommend that you play Good Night, Flashlight a few evenings prior to trying Flashlight Tag, because mastering how to track a moving point of light is easier while lying flat.)

Helps Your Child Develop and Enhance . . .
- Midline crossing (for tying shoes and buttoning cuffs)
- Motor planning (for moving through a crowded room)
- Visual tracking (for watching a puppet show)

What You Need
- Flashlight
- Lots of space to move in a darkened room

What You Do
1. In a darkened room, ask Joe to stand about six feet away from a wall. Shine your flashlight on the wall and say, "Joe, touch the light with your hand."
2. Move the light to several different spots, asking Joe to "tag" your light each time. Be sure to shine the light in such a way that Joe has to cross his midline in order to tag the light.
3. Slowly shine your light from side to side along the wall. Say, "Now I'm going to make it harder for you." Alternate between letting Joe tag the light and jerking it so it is just out of his reach. This switching tactic should elicit giggles.
4. Say, "Now I'm going to shine the light on the floor. Can you step on the light?" Shine the light slowly along the floor, again giving Joe several opportunities to tag it. Be sure to let him tag the light eventually.

5. Say, "Can you jump on the light with both feet?" as you quickly shine the light on the floor. As Joe jumps, move the light away so he just misses. Let him land on it successfully from time to time. Again, you should hear giggles galore!

Ways to Make It More Challenging

- Joe uses only his right (or left) hand (or foot) to tag the light.
- He alternates the hand (foot) he uses to tag the light. You may need to call out, "Right . . . left," to help him remember which hand to use.
- He uses both hands together to tag the light.

What to Look For

- Joe tags the light with the correct hand(s) or foot (feet).
- He alternates hands or feet correctly.
- He crosses his midline when necessary to tag the light.

GOOD NIGHT, FLASHLIGHT!

This interactive activity can be done at any time in a darkened room, and it is especially effective at bedtime, as it tends to be calming. Play Good Night, Flashlight! a few times before trying Flashlight Tag (page 70), because mastering how to track a moving point of light is easier while lying flat.

Helps Your Child Develop and Enhance . . .
- Bilateral coordination (for shrugging shoulders to say, "I don't know")
- Midline crossing (for shaking head no)
- Visual tracking (for watching the ice cream truck approach)

What You Need
- Two flashlights
- Darkened room
- Colored cellophane or filter to cover the glass, in order to differentiate the lights

What You Do
1. Have Annabel lie on her back on the floor or in bed.
2. Give Annabel a flashlight and ask her to hold it with two hands to promote midline crossing and bilateral coordination. Let her experiment with shining it on the ceiling, walls, and floor.
3. Then, very slowly, shine your light on the ceiling, moving from left to right. Say, "Annabel, now watch my light. Can you shine your light on mine?"
4. Move the light in straight or curved lines, primarily left to right and top to bottom (good training for learning to read).
5. Move the light in slow paths or "jump" it from place to place, requiring Annabel to shift her vision quickly.
6. Now let Annabel's light be the leader, while you shine your light on hers.
7. Say, "Annabel, watch my light. Make sure I'm staying on your light and doing a good job."

Ways to Make It More Challenging

- Change the speed of your flashlight path.
- "Draw" more intricate designs on the ceiling.
- Draw shapes or letters and ask Annabel to identify them.
- Ask Annabel to draw shapes or letters for you to identify.

What to Look For

- Annabel holds her flashlight with both hands.
- She beams her flashlight accurately.
- She is able to keep her light on yours for longer periods of time.

BECAUSE ENGLISH IS written and read from left to right, encourage Jessica to begin her eye tracking activities at the upper left. Dominoes and marble chutes offer additional opportunities for tracking practice, which may make learning to read easier.

GOPHER

While your little one pretends to be a curious gopher, this "baby" push-up is building his upper body strength and visual skills.

Helps Your Child Develop and Enhance . . .
- Bilateral coordination (for eating corn on the cob)
- Motor planning (for folding napkins)
- Proprioception (for peeling an orange)
- Visual skills (for setting the table)

What You Need
- Optional: metronome

What You Do
1. Ask Doug to lie on his stomach with his hands under his shoulders.
2. Say, "Doug, push your hands into the floor as you slowly raise your head. Keep your elbows on the floor. Look around, like a little gopher peeking out of his hole. Tell me what you see." (Be sure that Doug looks both right and left.)
3. Say, "Slowly, put your head down on the floor."
4. Repeat the exercise at least five times.
5. Optional: Lie on the floor, facing Doug, and do this activity together. Your heads should be about one foot apart when in the "down" position.

Ways to Make It More Challenging

- Doug raises and lowers himself to 4, 6, or 8 beats of a metronome set at 60 beats per minute.
- He focuses on a target when peeking from his "gopher hole."
- He does this activity on a less stable surface, such as a mattress or trampoline.

What to Look For

- Doug's movements are slow and even.
- He keeps his back as flat and still as he can.
- Both of his hands and knees remain on the floor.

HUG ROLL

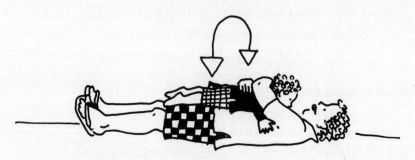

Rolling is one of the best activities for getting in touch with your own body. This rolling activity is interactive, as it requires a second roller. We suggest this on-the-spot remedy whether your child needs to rev up, stay tuned, or calm down.

Helps Your Child Develop and Enhance . . .
- Balance (for walking and climbing stairs)
- Motor planning (for crawling)
- Proprioception (for pushing open and holding a heavy door)
- Vestibular processing (for enjoying a merry-go-round)

What You Need
- Plenty of cushioned space on which to roll around together, such as a large gym mat, soft carpet, or mattress

What You Do
1. Lie on your back on the mat, or the floor, or the bed.
2. Say, "Chip, can you lie on me so that your tummy is touching my tummy?"
3. Say, "Now hug me tight," as you envelop Chip in a big bear hug.
4. Slowly roll over and over in a log roll, holding on to Chip so that he rolls with you. Be sure that his head is protected so that he never hyperextends his neck.
5. Be sure to roll in both directions.

Ways to Make It More Challenging

- Roll up an incline.
- Roll across a partially filled air mattress.

What to Look For

- Chip stays within your embrace throughout the roll.
- He tolerates the rolling motion.

IF I HAD A HAMMER

Kids love to hammer . . . in the morning, in the evening, all over this land! If I Had a Hammer lets them practice this valuable life skill in a safe environment. Your child needs to understand the rules of having a hammer in his hand. Make sure he stays in one spot to avoid the temptation of hitting everything and everyone in sight.

Helps Your Child Develop and Enhance . . .
- Laterality (for using the telephone)
- Proprioception (for inserting the key and unlocking the door)
- Tactile processing (for making mud pies and hamburger patties)
- Visual processing (for stepping onto an escalator)

What You Need
- Golf tees (or large nails)
- Wooden mallet (or toy hammer)
- Egg carton
- Foam block (packaging from a new appliance carton)
- Optional: tree stump

What You Do
1. Place the egg carton upside down and give Aaron a wooden mallet. Say, "Aaron, show me how you can hammer this egg carton flat."
2. Now put the foam block in front of Aaron and hand him a golf tee. Say, "Hold the golf tee in one hand and hit it into the foam block with your mallet."
3. Let him continue until he is tired.

Ways to Make It More Challenging
- Using colored golf tees and matching markers, play a matching game. Put colored dots on the egg carton, foam block, or tree stump, and ask Aaron to hammer the corresponding tees into the dots.

- Make a pattern of colored golf tees in the foam block and ask Aaron to copy it.
- Give Aaron nails, a tree stump, and a real hammer.

What to Look For
- Aaron pays attention to safety.
- He hits the golf tees and nails on the head.
- He matches the colors of golf tees and dots.
- He is able to reproduce your patterns.

OPPOSITES ATTRACT

Opposites Attract is based on an activity that is the cornerstone of the Brain Gym program (see www.braingym.org). This fun activity is easily adaptable for all ages and skill levels. Joye likes using this version as a warm-up at Kids Moving Company, because it integrates all the planes of the body—right and left, top and bottom, and forward and back.

Helps Your Child Develop and Enhance . . .
- Balance (for throwing while running)
- Body awareness (for pitching to the strike zone)
- Laterality (for sliding into home plate)
- Midline crossing (for swinging the bat)
- Motor planning (for swatting at flies and catching fly balls)
- Proprioception (for leaping up, reaching for, and catching the ball before it goes over the wall)

What You Need
- A place to stand

What You Do

1. Stand facing Sadie. Say, "Sadie, stand tall and look at me. Bring one knee up and touch it with your opposite hand." Demonstrating the movement for her is a good idea and will make you feel organized, too. If Sadie is unable to do this activity on her own, have her lie on her back while you move her body parts for her.

2. Say, "Now bring your other knee up and touch it with your opposite hand. Let's keep alternating hands and knees while we look at each other."

3. Say, "Sadie, raise one foot behind your back and touch it with your opposite hand. Now touch your other foot and hand." Continue alternating feet and hands for about 30 seconds.

Ways to Make It More Challenging

- Have Sadie begin by alternating her knees in front of her. When you say, "Back," have her switch to alternating her feet behind her. When you say, "Front," have her switch again to knees in front.
- Introduce a pattern, such as, "Three front, two back," or "Four front, one back." (When designing your pattern, use an odd number of repeats to be sure Sadie begins on a different knee each time she switches.)
- Have her move forward and backward as she maintains the pattern.
- Have Sadie spell her name, address, telephone number, or spelling words as she maintains the pattern.
- To add another level of difficulty, have Sadie spell her name beginning with her knees in front, and as she comes to each vowel, have her switch to feet in back.

What to Look For

- Sadie stands up tall throughout the activity.
- She looks at you, not at the floor.
- She is able to switch smoothly and accurately from forward to back to forward again.

PILLOW PILE

Does your "little monkey" love jumping on the bed? Jumping is terrific, especially when enjoyed in a *safe* environment. So, arrange a mound of pillows in a spacious room for a joyful leap-and-land experience. Leaping onto a Pillow Pile can be energizing or calming, depending on the time of day and your child's state. Then, instead of "No more monkeys jumping on the bed!" you can say, "Go for it!"

Helps Your Child Develop and Enhance . . .
- Proprioception (for endurance and "oomph")
- Vestibular processing (for learning how to tumble and fall safely)
- Motor planning (for figuring out how to stop and go)

What You Need
- Soft pile to jump into, such as:
  - Pile of bed pillows and couch cushions, covered and loosely held together with a bed sheet, or
  - Jumping pad, made by stuffing old pillows and blocks of upholstery foam into a king-size duvet cover
- Sufficient space for running toward the pile, or furniture to jump from
- Optional: large beach ball

What You Do
1. Ask Pearl to stand about 10 feet away from the prepared mound of pillows. Say, "Show me how you can run and land on the Pillow Pile."
2. Alternatively, have Pearl stand on a couch and jump into the pile.

Ways to Make It More Challenging

- Have Pearl move slowly, quickly, or turning in circles toward the pile.
- Have her show you her own ways to move toward the pile and fall into it.
- Just as she is ready to jump, toss a large, soft ball for her to catch.

What to Look For

- Pearl runs and jumps in one fluid movement.
- She can wriggle her way out of the Pillow Pile independently.

RED CUP, BLUE CUP

Besides being just plain fun, Red Cup, Blue Cup also develops sensory, perceptual, and visual skills. Even older children will find this activity challenging outside of the bathtub when you use the suggestions listed below in "Ways to Make It More Challenging."

Helps Your Child Develop and Enhance . . .

- Midline crossing (for playing Ping-Pong and badminton)
- Motor planning (for getting on and off a horse)
- Proprioception (for orienting your limbs to get dressed and go dancing)
- Spatial awareness (for judging how much milk will fit in your cup)
- Visual tracking (for scanning a room to find your backpack and scanning a shelf to find a book)

What You Need

- A blue and a red plastic cup, or any two different-colored plastic cups
- Bathtub filled with water

What You Do

1. When Thea is in the bathtub, hand her a blue cup and let her play with it, filling it and pouring the water out.

2. Give her the red cup and say, "Show me how you pour the water from the blue cup into the red cup." (Thea will probably pour at her midline.)

3. Hold your hands up in front of you, about one foot apart. Say, "Thea, look at my hands. Now move your hands apart, just like mine." You may need to position her hands for her, until she gets the idea.

4. Each time she pours, encourage her to gradually expand the distance between her hands, until her cups are shoulder-width apart from each other.

5. As she begins to pour from the blue to the red cup, her instinct may be to bring the red cup in close to her midline. Remind her: "Keep the red cup *way* near the wall. Keep it very still and bring the blue cup *way* over to it."

6. Have her switch the cups, so she crosses the midline with the other hand.

Ways to Make It More Challenging

- Have Thea do Red Cup, Blue Cup at the sink, because standing is harder than sitting.
- Fill the cups with beans instead of water and have Thea do the pouring at a table, while seated.
- Have her stand on a balance board while pouring beans.

What to Look For

- Thea pours the water (beans) with minimal spillage.
- She looks at her hands and watches as she pours.
- She holds the red cup still and brings the blue cup to it across her midline.
- She holds the waiting cup out to the side of her body, rather than at the midline.

SCOOTIE CUTIE

Numerous activities can be performed on a scooter board, which can be made easily by a handy person or purchased. The board should be approximately 12 inches square with good-quality casters mounted on each of the four corners. The board can be covered with carpet to make it more comfortable.

This activity is a blast! Try it—you will see what we mean.

Helps Your Child Develop and Enhance . . .
- Bilateral coordination (for playing the accordion)
- Laterality (for conducting the orchestra)
- Motor planning (for playing the cello)
- Proprioception (for playing chords on a guitar or piano)

What You Need
- Scooter board
- Visual target
- Smooth floor surface
- Optional: masking tape, obstacles, or long rope

What You Do
1. Let Dawn experiment with the scooter board, discovering all the ways she can move. For safety reasons, do not allow her to stand on it.

2. Say, "Dawn, lay your tummy on the scooter and pull and push yourself around using just your hands. No elbows, no feet! Try using both hands at the same time. Now try using one hand at a time."
3. Say, "Dawn, sit on the scooter and push yourself around using your feet. Can you do it using both feet at the same time? How about pushing with just one foot at a time?"

Ways to Make It More Challenging

- Make an obstacle course for Dawn to maneuver around, in various positions on the scooter board.
- Lay a masking tape path on the floor for Dawn to follow.
- Hold one end of a long rope and give her the other end. Ask her to pull herself to you, hand over hand, until she can touch your shoe.
- Have her lie with her stomach on the scooter board and her feet flat against a wall. Have her straighten her knees and legs quickly, giving herself sudden acceleration. How far can she go? Whee!

What to Look For

- Dawn looks at the target as much as possible while moving.
- She uses both hands together when appropriate, or both feet.
- She alternates hands or feet when appropriate.
- She has the strength to propel her body across the floor.

SUPERKID

Playing this uplifting game, your child feels truly super, because he is "flying" like a superhero; because it is exciting to be over and above you, as the Latin word "super" implies; and because the activity is simply superlative fun! This is an ideal In-Sync activity for little kids who love to defy gravity and for adults who have superstrong legs.

Helps Your Child Develop and Enhance . . .
- Balance (for staying centered on a rocking horse)
- Bilateral coordination (for using both hands and feet to hang on to a rocking horse)
- Motor planning (for getting on and off a rocking horse)
- Proprioception (for making a rocking horse rock)
- Vestibular processing (for riding a rocking horse without falling off)

What You Need
- Adult with strong legs
- Comfortable space to lie down

What You Do
1. Lie on your back and ask Elliot to stand in front of your feet, facing you.
2. Gently place the soles of your feet on Elliot's stomach. Say, "Elliot, give me your hands."
3. Hold Elliot's hands and slowly extend your legs until Elliot is over your body, parallel to the floor.
4. Say, "Elliot, stretch out your legs in a straight line behind you. Now you're flying like Superman!"

Ways to Make It More Challenging

- Gently bend and straighten your legs for an up-and-down ride.
- Have Elliot let go of your hands while "flying."
- Have Elliot keep his legs straight and then extend his arms in a T-formation, holding the position for a few seconds.

What to Look For

- Elliot is evenly balanced on your feet.
- He maintains an extended position, holding his head up and legs out.
- He is comfortable being passively moved when you shift your legs beneath him.
- He enjoys being up off the ground.

WHEELBARROW

When your child wobbles like a wheelbarrow down the garden path or hallway, she will be able to mark her progress as she gets stronger and travels farther. The first time, she gets as far as the rock; the second time, the tree; the third time, the fence. How satisfying!

Helps Your Child Develop and Enhance . . .
- Motor planning (for getting through the school day)
- Proprioception (for sensing how tightly to hold a pencil)
- Vestibular processing (for sitting at a desk)

What You Need
- Visual target, such as a twig or doorway
- Space to move

What You Do
1. Ask Jenny to put her hands on the floor.
2. Put a visual target in front of Jenny at her eye level, at least 8 to 10 feet away.
3. Stand behind Jenny and pick up both her legs, holding them between the ankles and the knees. (You may need to do this exercise on *your* knees, so you don't put a strain on Jenny's back.)
4. Say, "Move forward on your hands toward the target. Keep looking at the target."
5. As Jenny gets stronger, she will do more of the work, and you will do less.

Ways to Make It More Challenging
- Make a path on the floor using masking tape.
- Build a mini–obstacle course for Jenny to move through.
- Have her go backward.

What to Look For

- Jenny's hands are flat and facing forward.
- She looks at the target the whole time.
- She does not sink onto her elbows.

KIDS WANT AND need to do real work! For many children, work is play. Offer them the chance to do heavy-work activities that involve pushing, pulling, lifting, and carrying. Examples are pushing a friend on the swing, pulling a rake, lifting groceries from cart to car, or carrying the laundry basket upstairs. Whether your child has low stamina or is constantly on the go, heavy-work activities are therapeutically sound for all.

Intermediate Activities

ANGEL WINGS

This activity provides a feel-good-all-over stretch. Have your child do it in the sand, in the snow, or on a carpet with a plush nap, so that when he stands up, he can marvel at the impression of his glorious wings.

Helps Your Child Develop and Enhance . . .
- Proprioception (for pulling on socks and pushing open doors)
- Bilateral coordination (for clapping, jumping, and other two-sided activities)
- Laterality (for crawling and running)
- Motor planning (for making your body do what you want, such as getting in and out of tight spaces)
- Binocularity (for using both eyes together to judge depth and distance)

What You Need
- Visual target on the ceiling, such as a light fixture
- Metronome (for the most difficult sequence)

What You Do
1. Say, "Lie on the floor, on your back. Put your hands at your sides. Bring your legs together. Look at the light fixture on the ceiling."
2. Say, "Pretend your arms are long Angel Wings." Touch Isaac's right arm as you say, "Slowly move your right wing along the floor until it is straight over your head. Now move it slowly back to your side."
3. Say, "Do it again, three more times."
4. Have Isaac repeat the movements, with these body parts (three times each), in this order:
   - Right arm
   - Left arm
   - Both arms together, smoothly and simultaneously

- Right leg
- Left leg
- Both legs together, smoothly and simultaneously
- Right arm and right leg together
- Left arm and left leg together
- Right arm and left leg together
- Left arm and right leg together

5. Have Isaac repeat the sequence, making each movement twice.
6. Have Isaac repeat the sequence, making each movement once.

Ways to Make It More Challenging

- Have Isaac make the movements to verbal cues only, without your helpful touches.
- Have Isaac make the movements without verbal cues, so he relies on his own memory.
- Have Isaac make each movement to your claps or to a metronome set at about 60 beats per minute. Remember: Slowly is best!

What to Look For

- Isaac moves only the arm or leg called for.
- Isaac fully extends each limb, smoothly and easily.
- When moving two limbs, Isaac moves them at the same time.

ARM CIRCLES

Here's a perfect quickie activity to use as a movement break at school or home. It is easy, feels good, and is therapeutic for the body and brain. A few minutes of Arm Circles will give your child a chance to breathe deeply and stretch widely, to "get the kinks out," and then to settle down and focus on homework. Try it—it works like magic.

Helps Your Child Develop and Enhance . . .
- Bilateral coordination (for holding and passing a beach ball)
- Motor planning (for moving and writing easily)
- Proprioception (for lifting the laundry basket and carrying it upstairs)

What You Need
- No equipment

What You Do
1. Have Malia stand in a space where she can extend her arms easily. Say, "Extend your arms to the sides and rotate them in small circles, ten times."
2. Say, "Now reverse direction, and rotate your arms ten times."

Ways to Make It More Challenging

- Have Malia make Arm Circles above her head.
- Have Malia make Arm Circles in front of her body.

What to Look For

- Malia's arms stay extended throughout the activity.
- She simultaneously moves both arms.
- She is consistent in the size and direction of her Arm Circles.
- She switches direction accurately.

BACK DRAWING

Everyone needs to touch and be touched, but some kids will resist hugs and kisses. This activity is a delightful opportunity to get close to your child and at the same time to strengthen his letter recognition and other perceptual skills.

Helps Your Child Develop and Enhance . . .
- Directionality (for understanding right/left and up/down)
- Spatial awareness (for maneuvering through obstacles and moving through a crowded space)
- Tactile processing (for wearing differently textured clothes)
- Visual processing (for envisioning letters and shapes)

What You Need
- No equipment

What You Do
1. Ask Amiel to sit on a chair with his back facing you.
2. Say, "I'm going to draw a shape on your back. Can you tell me what it is?"
3. With your finger, draw a circle on Amiel's back. (If he is ticklish, draw firmly. Light, unexpected touch may irritate children who are easily overstimulated by touch sensations. Firm touch is usually more acceptable.) Say, "What did I draw?"
4. If Amiel does not know, draw a circle again until he recognizes the shape.

Ways to Make It More Challenging
- Have your child draw the shape on your back.
- Draw shapes such as triangles, ovals, hearts, and stars.
- Draw letters or numbers.

What to Look For
- Amiel correctly identifies the shape.
- He tolerates the sensation of your drawing on his back.

BALL BOUNCE

TAPE LINE

Wannabe basketball players will think this activity is cool, as it is excellent practice for dribbling a ball around the court. Even *don't* wannabe basketball players will like it!

Helps Your Child Develop and Enhance . . .
- Balance (for catching oneself when falling)
- Bilateral coordination (for pumping one's legs and holding on when swinging)
- Laterality (for walking and knowing right from left)
- Midline crossing (for scratching one's elbow and crossing one's legs)
- Motor planning (for doing homework and getting dressed)
- Proprioception (for waving a flag and peeling a banana)

What You Need
- Playground ball
- Masking tape
- Optional: metronome, tennis ball, balance beam

What You Do

1. Give Noah the ball and have him practice bouncing and catching it with both hands.
2. Put a long line of masking tape on the floor. Say, "Can you walk on this tape while bouncing and catching the ball? Remember to use both hands."
3. Say, "This time, take a step and bounce the ball to the left of the tape. Take another step and bounce the ball to the right of the tape. Keep going."

Ways to Make It More Challenging

- Have Noah do the activity backward.
- Have him bounce the ball to a metronome beat.
- Have him use a tennis ball instead of a bigger ball.
- Have him do the activity on a balance beam.

What to Look For

- Noah uses both hands to bounce and catch the ball.
- Both of his feet stay on the tape as he bounces and catches the ball.
- Noah remembers to alternate sides.

BUS DRIVER

Most children are very excited to ride on the big yellow school bus. This game lets your child be both bus driver and passenger. As the driver, he will take you for a slow or speedy, straight or curvy ride around the yard. As the passenger, he will soon learn to control the bus's direction and velocity from the "backseat."

Helps Your Child Develop and Enhance . . .
- Motor planning (for stowing your backpack and lunch box)
- Proprioception (for getting on a bus and hanging on to the pole)
- Vestibular processing (for staying on your feet when the bus turns a corner)
- Visual processing (for picking out an empty seat on the crowded bus)

What You Need
- Bicycle tube (free from the bike shop), with metal valve snipped out (a hula hoop is fun, too, but does not provide the resistive, stretchy quality of a tube)
- Plenty of space to run around
- Optional: small hoop or paper plate for the steering wheel

What You Do

1. Show the bike tube to Frankie and say, "Let's play Bus Driver. We both need to step into this circle. Do you want to be the driver or the passenger?"
2. If Frankie chooses to be the driver, say, "Put the tube across your tummy." When it is his turn to be the passenger, say, "Put the tube behind your back" (at the waist). "Pretend the tube is a seat belt. Hold on to it so it doesn't fall down."
3. If he is the driver, say, "Drive!" Or if you are the driver, say, "Hang on to your seat belt! Here we go!"
4. Drive around the yard together. As the driver, Frankie will take you for a joyful ride as he pulls you around. As the passenger, he will delight in slowing you down when he pulls back and in changing your direction when he presses on the right or left side of the tube to rein you in.

Ways to Make It More Challenging

- Give Frankie a hoop or paper plate to be the driver's steering wheel. To steer with it, he must let go of the seat belt and use his hips to keep the tube from relaxing and falling down.
- Experiment with Frankie by winding inside the circle, rotating from belly to back against the resistive tube.

What to Look For

- Frankie is able to pull his weight against the resistance of the tube.
- As the passenger, he keeps his balance.
- As the driver, he slows down and corrects his direction when approaching trees, fences, or other obstacles.

CAN'T TAP ME

This giggly game is a classic "twosie." At the same time that child and grown-up are having fun, they are also crossing the midline. Crossing the midline is an important ability for moving smoothly in hundreds of ways throughout the day. This game also develops a good sense of timing. (Joye calls this game Strawberries because that's what her grandfather called it.)

Helps Your Child Develop and Enhance . . .
- Midline crossing (for steering a bumper car)
- Motor planning (for tying shoes and cutting with scissors)
- Tactile processing (for interpreting a gentle touch accurately)
- Visual tracking (for reading)

What You Need
- Just the two of you, facing each other

What You Do
1. Face Jack and extend your hands, palms up. Say, "Place your hands lightly on top of mine, palms down."
2. Say, "I'll try to tap your hand, and you try to pull it away before I can. Are you ready?" Quickly bring your right hand out from under Jack's left hand, cross your midline, and tap the back of his right hand.
3. Return to the starting position. Now try to tap Jack's left hand with your left hand.
4. Repeat until Jack succeeds in pulling away a hand before you can tap it. (You can slow down to let him succeed.)

Ways to Make It More Challenging
- Let Jack be the tapper, and you, the "tappee."
- Fake it. Move one hand slightly but do not actually take it out from under Jack's hand.

What to Look For

- Jack anticipates your movements and moves his hands accordingly.
- He crosses his midline rather than turning his whole body to tap your hand.

HAND DOMINANCE USUALLY is established by age six. To help Ned's brain "decide" which hand will be dominant, it is helpful to hand things to him at his midline. Then, Ned can choose which hand to use, rather than simply using the hand closest to yours.

CAT BALANCE SEQUENCE

Getting into "cat position" is an exercise in itself. Before you begin the activity, have your child arch and then round her spine a few times for a feel-good stretch. For younger kids, have them raise their "paws." For older kids, simply use the word "hands."

Helps Your Child Develop and Enhance . . .
- Balance (for walking on the curb)
- Laterality (for knowing right and left on one's own body)
- Motor planning (for carrying out a complex sequence of unfamiliar movements)
- Vestibular processing (for moving without getting dizzy)

What You Need
- Visual target, for example, a picture of a kitten, at eye level when child is in "cat" position
- Metronome (for most challenging sequence)

What You Do
1. Say, "Get into cat position," helping Leah, if necessary, to place her hands and knees on the floor with her hands flat and her fingers facing forward.
2. Say, "Look at the picture of the cat. Raise one paw (or, "Raise your right paw") just a little bit off the floor. Let's count slowly to five."

3. Repeat:
   - Left paw
   - Right knee
   - Left knee
   - Right paw, right knee ("Raise one paw and the knee on the same side." Touch the child's hand and knee, if necessary.)
   - Left paw, left knee
   - Right paw, left knee ("Raise a paw on one side and the opposite knee," or "Raise your right paw and left knee.")
   - Left paw, right knee

Ways to Make It More Challenging

- Have Leah count by herself.
- Set metronome to 50 to 70 beats a minute, using the visual option. Have Leah do the activity while watching the light flash on the metronome and counting aloud.
- Using the metronome, have Leah count and remember the hand-and-knee sequence without your coaching.

What to Look For

- Leah keeps her back straight and parallel to the floor. It is usually easier to maintain a flat back when lifting either hand than when lifting a knee.
- She focuses on the cat picture throughout the activity.

CHALKBOARD CIRCLE

This activity exercises the important visual skill of tracking. As you will recall, tracking is moving your eyes smoothly in a line, such as when reading, watching a bird in flight . . . or drawing circles on a chalkboard. Chalkboard Circle is a more "grown-up" activity than Roundabout (page 146), although the movements are similar.

Helps Your Child Develop and Enhance . . .
- Midline crossing (for hitting the baseball or golf ball)
- Motor planning (for coordinating eyes and hands for handwriting and drawing)
- Visual tracking (for watching where the baseball or golf ball goes)

What You Need
- Chalkboard, or a large piece of paper taped to the wall
- Chalk or crayon
- Optional: telephone book

What You Do

1. Draw a small "X" on the board or paper in front of Marvin's nose.
2. Give Marvin the chalk or a crayon and ask him to draw a large circle around the "X," at least 12 inches in diameter. To encourage him to move toward his midline, if he is right-handed have him move his hand counterclockwise, and if he is left-handed, have him move his hand clockwise.
3. Now ask him to place his chalk or crayon at the top of his circle and draw another circle exactly on it. Say, "Go slowly, so you stay on the line."

Ways to Make It More Challenging

- Put a beanbag on Marvin's head to encourage him to keep his head still and move only his eyes.
- Have him stand on a telephone book to encourage him to stay in one place, which will allow him to cross the midline.
- Have him switch the direction of his circle drawing.

What to Look For

- Marvin draws toward the midline—that is, from the side toward the center of his body. If he is right-handed, he draws counterclockwise. If he is left-handed, he draws clockwise.
- He stands squarely in front of the circle the whole time.
- His second circle is directly on top of the first one.

CRAYONS ARE A great tool for developing tactile and proprioceptive skills. Crayons encourage Lily to use fine motor muscles in her hands and fingers to bear down firmly in order to produce color. Crayons also allow Lily the opportunity to decide whether to produce dark or light color tones. Markers don't have these advantages.

DRUMROLL, PLEASE

This activity is about moving in specific ways to specific sounds produced by different rhythm band instruments, homemade instruments, or *your* hands and feet. In this activity, sounds, rather than words, tell your child how to move. Some children may find it very easy, while others will find it quite challenging.

Helps Your Child Develop and Enhance . . .
- Balance (for hopping and marching)
- Bilateral coordination (for clapping and jumping)
- Spatial awareness (for playing Hide-and-Seek)

What You Need
- Sound makers, such as:
  - Drum and drumsticks, or oatmeal box and chopsticks
  - Shaker, or beans in a plastic tub
  - Rhythm sticks, or wooden spoons
  - Sand blocks, or two paper plates
  - Clapping hands
  - Stomping feet
- Open space in which to move

What You Do
1. On the board, make a grid with two columns: "Sound" and "Movement."
2. Say, "Madeline, I am going to make different sounds. Each sound will tell you how to move. When I beat the drum slowly (or, "When I clap slowly . . ."), that sound tells you to walk slowly around the room. Listen."
3. Beat the drum slowly with your hand (or clap slowly), while Madeline walks around the room.

4. Now beat the drum quickly. Ask Madeline, "What would be a good way of moving to this drumbeat? Ah, you think running would be good? I think so, too! Go!" (For inspiration, see the table below.)
5. Say, "Now I'm going to use two drumsticks to play a drumroll." (Beat the drum quickly, right-left-right-left.) "Madeline, when you hear a drumroll, get down on the floor and roll."
6. Continue to make different sounds. With Madeline, decide on an appropriate form of locomotion for each sound. (The first time you do this activity, three or four sounds and movements will be sufficient.)

Ways to Make It More Challenging
- Increase the number of sound-and-movement pairs.
- Move out of sight, so Madeline must recognize the sounds using only her ears without the help of vision.
- Have Madeline play the instruments or make the sounds with her own body, while you respond with the moves.

What to Look For
- Madeline responds quickly to the changing sounds.
- She matches her movements to the sounds.
- Her movements are fluid and efficient.

EXAMPLES OF SOUNDS AND WAYS TO MOVE

Sound	Movement
Slow drumbeat (Slow clapping)	Walk slowly
Fast drumbeat (Fast clapping)	Run
Drumroll (Foot stomping)	Roll
Shaker	Shake hands in the air
Rhythm sticks	Gallop, jump
Sand blocks	Skate

EYE SPY

Eye Spy is based on a visual training activity that many developmental optometrists have found beneficial. Optometrists refer to the chart as the "OAT (Ocular-Auditory-Transfer) Chart." A fun way to personalize this activity is to use photographs or pictures instead of the alphabet to design the chart. Or you can use a combination of pictures, letters, and numbers.

Helps Your Child Develop and Enhance . . .

- Directionality (for crossing the playground on the diagonal)
- Vestibular processing (for standing while following verbal directions)
- Visual tracking (for reading and sports)

What You Need

- Chalkboard or poster board with a grid of sixteen squares, each about 4 by 4 inches. Write a letter, integer, or symbol in each square.

What You Do

1. Place the board at Annie's eye level and ask her to stand or sit so she can touch the chart. Say, "Look at the chart and point to the letter B (number 2, smiley face, etc.)."

2. Say, "Move your finger two squares to the right. What letter are you on?" If Annie doesn't yet know right and left, gesture toward the direction in which you want her to move her finger.

3. Repeat, asking Annie to move her finger along the chart, in all directions, for example:
   - Three squares to the left
   - One square up
   - Two squares down

4. Once Annie can do this with ease, ask her to stand or sit, with both feet on the floor, about 8 to 10 feet away from the chart.

5. Say, "Look at the letter B. Move just your eyes two squares to the right. Keep your head very still. What letter are your eyes on?"

Ways to Make It More Challenging

- Use two-step directions ("Move two to the right and one down") or three-step directions ("Move two to the left, one down, and two to the right").
- Have Annie stand on a balance board while looking at the chart.
- Have her give the directions to you. Give a wrong answer occasionally to make sure that she is really watching the chart.

What to Look For

- Annie uses only her eyes without moving her head.
- She responds quickly and moves her eyes *at the same time* as the directions are given.

DO YOU SEE Robyn resting her head on her arm, desk, or even the floor when she is writing or coloring? This could be due to incorrect table height, low muscle tone, or just because . . . In this position, Robyn is forced to use only one eye. If she were to use both her eyes, she would have double vision, so her brain turns off one image. If Robyn's brain does this too often, she may develop amblyopia. Always encourage Robyn to color, read, and write in an upright position.

FLASHLIGHT FOCUS

Once your child gets into the swing of this activity, the rhythm is very organizing. It is an interesting way to move from Point A to Point B—such as down the corridor from one room to another, or from the house to the mailbox—and of course, it's fun, too.

Helps Your Child Develop and Enhance . . .
- Laterality (for developing a hand preference)
- Midline crossing (for kicking a ball and getting dressed)
- Visual tracking (for keeping one's place while reading)

What You Need
- Two flashlights
- Space to walk
- Optional: metronome

What You Do
1. Give Melissa one flashlight to hold in her right hand. Say, "Walk slowly across the room. Every time your left foot goes forward, shine the light on it."
2. Ask Melissa to put the flashlight in her left hand and shine the light on her right foot as she walks back to the starting point.

3. Give her the second flashlight so she holds one in each hand. Say, "Walk slowly and focus a light on a foot each time you take a step. Remember which light shines on which foot."

Ways to Make It More Challenging
- Ask Melissa to walk to a slow metronome beat, about 44 per minute.
- Ask her to do the activity walking backward.

What to Look For
- Melissa stands up straight with good posture as she shines the light on her foot.
- She aims the light accurately.

FLIP FLOP

Flip Flop is one of Joye's favorite In-Sync activities. She begins almost every therapy session with it. The ability to make these seemingly simple switches is crucial to learning how to live in one's body comfortably.

Helps Your Child Develop and Enhance . . .
- Body awareness (for getting fingers into gloves or thumbs into mittens)
- Laterality (for pointing)
- Motor planning (for playing Cat's Cradle)
- Proprioception (for getting arms into sleeves of jackets and coats)

What You Need
- Mat or comfortable place to lie down

What You Do
1. Ask Kelly-Ann to lie on her stomach with arms at her sides. Say, "Bend your knee up to your side. Keep your foot on the mat." (You may need to position her leg.)

2. Say, "Place your opposite hand on the mat above your head." (Position her arm, if necessary.)

3. Say, "Now turn your head so that you are looking at your elbow."

4. Say, "Keeping your head and arms in place, straighten your bent leg and bend your straight leg. Now switch again." Have Kelly-Ann repeat this switching movement until she is comfortable with it.

5. Say, "Now hold your legs still and switch your arms while you turn your head." Again, have Kelly-Ann repeat this movement until she is comfortable with it.

6. Say, "Now put it all together and switch everything at the same time." Once Kelly-Ann is successful, build up to ten repetitions.

Ways to Make It More Challenging

- Have Kelly-Ann start with her leg and arm bent on the same side, and her head facing the same direction.
- Have her start with her arm and leg bent on one side, with her head facing the other direction.

IMPORTANT: Always end Flip Flop with at least six repetitions of the original position.

What to Look For

- Kelly-Ann's movements are smooth and integrated.
- She is able to maintain correct positions as she switches her arms and legs.

WHENEVER ZAK ALTERNATES the two sides of his body, he is enhancing his laterality.

FOLLOW THE FEATHER

Follow the Feather, another eye-tracking activity, gives kids an opportunity to use their eyes as Mother Nature intended. In addition, because feathers move in the air *very slowly*, children have ample time to motor plan to catch their feather before it touches the ground.

Helps Your Child Develop and Enhance . . .
- Balance (for staying upright)
- Body awareness (for dressing paper dolls)
- Midline crossing (for sweeping and raking)
- Motor planning (for coordinating one movement with another)
- Visual tracking (for watching a tennis match)

What You Need
- A few feathers

What You Do
1. Let Ruthie choose a feather. Ask her to stroke it on her:
   - Arms
   - Legs
   - Cheeks
2. Have her balance the feather on:
   - Her foot
   - The back of her hand
   - Her nose
3. Say, "Hold your feather way up high in the air. Now let it go and watch it as it falls slowly to the floor."
4. Say, "Hold your feather way up high again. Now let it go and catch it . . ." Have her catch it:
   - On the back of her hand
   - On her foot
   - With both hands

Ways to Make It More Challenging

- Have Ruthie hold her feather way up high, let it go, and then:
  - Sit down first and catch it.
  - Spin around and catch it.
  - Clap her hands and catch it.
- Say, "Hold your feather way up high in the air." Ask her if she can keep it up in the air by:
  - Blowing on it.
  - Clapping her hands under it.
  - Swishing her hands back and forth under it.

What to Look For

- Ruthie uses the correct body part as requested.
- She makes all the moves with efficient motor planning and coordination, perhaps after a few tries for the more complex commands.

HEADS UP, TOES DOWN

Got one drowsy kid or a classroom full of fidgety kids? Need a quick stretching activity to liven up the drowsy and calm the restless? Want to teach basic skills, such as body parts and the concept of up and down? Want to teach academic skills, such as musical concepts and math facts? While you're at it, want to include a midline-crossing activity and maybe a bit of rhyming? All in 15 seconds? This activity takes the prize!

Helps Your Child Develop and Enhance . . .
- Bilateral coordination (for pulling up her pants)
- Body awareness (for getting her heels into her socks)
- Spatial awareness (for moving safely through space)

What You Need
- Xylophone and mallet, or keyboard

What You Do
1. Show the xylophone (or keyboard) and say, "A musical scale is like a ladder. You can climb up, step by step. Watch and listen as the mallet climbs up the musical scale." Hit the lowest, largest tone on the xylophone (or middle C on the keyboard) and slowly play and sing, "One, two, three, four, five, six, seven, eight." If you can't carry a tune in a bucket, just say the numbers in a gradually rising voice: "One" is in your lowest voice; "eight" is in your highest.

2. Say, "Now Becky, you sing the numbers with me." Play up the scale again.
3. Play down the scale, singing in reverse from "eight" to "one."
4. Say, "Becky, now put your hands on the floor (or on your knees) and move your hands step by step, little by little, as we sing up and down the scale."

Ways to Make It More Challenging
- Replace the numbers (one through eight) with:
  - The eight letter names of the musical notes: C, D, E, F, G, A, B, C
  - The musical syllables: Do, Re, Mi, Fa, So, La, Ti, Do
  - Eight body parts, for example, heels, ankles, knees, thighs, hips, ribs, shoulders, head
- Reverse the direction, going down the body instead of working your way up.
- Repeat variations as a midline-crossing exercise, with hands crossed.
- Have Becky lie on her back and repeat variations, raising legs instead of arms.

What to Look For
- Becky moves her body parts upward and then downward with a smooth, fluid quality.
- She moves slowly, in sync with you and any others playing this up-down game, without rushing to "win."
- She simultaneously moves and sings or says appropriate words.

HIP, HIP, HOORAY!

Rolling, rolling, and more rolling is good for *everybody*. Rolling delivers important sensory input to the skin, inner ear, muscles, and joints. Rolling is also an easy and manageable activity that even children who fear movement can do successfully. Do this activity on a level surface rather than on a hill. Make sure your child rolls an equal number of times in both directions.

Helps Your Child Develop and Enhance . . .
- Body awareness (for playing Simon Says and Head, Shoulders, Knees, and Toes)
- Motor planning (for organizing one's actions in a purposeful way)
- Proprioception (for orienting one's limbs to get dressed)
- Vestibular processing (for enjoying merry-go-rounds and swinging)

What You Need
- Plenty of cushioned, level space, free of obstacles, on carpet, a large mat, or grass

What You Do
1. Ask Luke to lie on his back. Say, "Roll from here to there" (at least eight feet). "Now roll back to me."
2. Say, "This time, lead with your shoulder and roll to there. Make sure your shoulder goes first, each time you roll. Now roll back to me the same way." Luke may need you to touch his shoulder in order to start.

3. Be sure Luke rolls in both directions as he leads with his:
   - Head
   - Hips
   - Knees
4. Say, "This last time, show me how you can roll with everything together."

Ways to Make It More Challenging
- None, as this one is hard enough on its own.

What to Look For
- Luke locates his shoulder, head, hips, and knees without your help.
- He uses the body part requested to start his roll and to continue with each flip.

KEYBOARD TALES

Here's a novel way to retell familiar tales, using a piano instead of a picture book. One of Carol's favorites, Keyboard Tales amuses children who have good language skills as well as those whose language skills are still developing. Indeed, some kids may find that "letting their fingers do the talking" is quite refreshing, especially if they are the children who hear grown-ups constantly commenting, "Use your words" and "Good talking!"

Helps Your Child Develop and Enhance . . .
- Bilateral coordination (for playing Patty-Cake and other "twosie" clapping rhymes)
- Directionality (for finding the starting point of a sentence or a workbook maze)
- Midline crossing (for paddling a canoe)
- Motor planning (for getting things into and out of a backpack)
- Proprioception (for knowing when to press hard or lightly on a crayon or pencil)

What You Need
- Piano or electronic keyboard with at least four octaves
- Nursery tales or familiar storybooks, such as:

Stories with 2 or 3 Voices	Stories with 4 or 5 Voices
Caps for Sale, by Slobodkina	*Goldilocks and the Three Bears*
Little Miss Muffet (Spider says, "Hi!")	*The Three Little Pigs*
The Runaway Bunny, by Brown	*Little Red Riding Hood*
Swimmy, by Lionni	*The Gingerbread Man*
Frog and Toad Are Friends, by Lobel	*The Bremen Town Musicians*

What You Do

1. Stand on Gordon's right at the piano and say, "Gordon, let's tell *Goldilocks and the Three Bears* on the keyboard."

2. Show Gordon four ranges on the keyboard where the four story characters "speak."

   - Strike a few bass (low) notes at the far left of the keyboard. In a low, loud voice, say, "This is how Papa Bear sounds when he talks."
   - Play a few notes an octave or two higher, but below middle C. Say in a regular, adult voice, "This is how Mama Bear sounds."
   - Play a few notes above middle C. In a girl's voice, say, "This is Goldilocks."
   - Play a few treble (high) notes lightly at the far right and say in a high, babyish voice, "And this is how Baby Bear sounds."

3. Have Gordon sit at the center of the keyboard, in front of middle C. Have him use both hands to play each character's "voice."

4. Begin telling the story. When a character speaks, have Gordon accompany the words by pounding on—or tickling—the ivories in the appropriate range.

Ways to Make It More Challenging

- Gordon speaks the character's lines while he plays the piano keys.
- He uses only his right hand to play Papa Bear and Mama Bear's voices, and only his left hand to play Goldilocks and Baby Bear's voices.
- He makes up his own Keyboard Tales.

ook For

- crosses the midline easily.
- loud and soft playing as appropriate.
- he story characters appropriately on the low,
- gh ranges of the keyboard.

WHENEVER READING WITH Marian, be sure to sit on her right side. For most of us, reading is usually easier when the material is placed to the right of our midline. Sitting next to Marian on the couch, you will tend to place the written material where it is easiest for you to process. Give Marian's developing brain a head start. Let her perceive the written words where it is easiest for her to process them.

LOOK MA, NO HANDS!

Ah, the paper plate! Such a simple object, so many fun ways to use it! Look Ma, No Hands! can be played anywhere your child has room to move. It requires your child to use his whole body *except for* his hands. This activity, too, can be done alone or with a friend.

Helps Your Child Develop and Enhance . . .
- Body awareness (for recognizing and moving various body parts)
- Motor planning (for learning dance steps and yoga poses)
- Laterality (for highlighting words on a page and turning pages in a book)
- Proprioception (for screwing and unscrewing a jar lid)

What You Need
- One paper plate
- Ample space to move
- Optional: obstacles and tape

What You Do
1. Give Matthew the paper plate. Say, "Show me how you can walk across the room balancing the plate on your head. Do not let your hands touch the plate."
2. Ask Matthew to show you a way to move the plate across the room using:
   - Elbows only
   - Knees only
   - Ear and shoulder together
   - Knee and elbow together
   - Chin only
   - Pointy or round parts of his body
   - Three, four, or five parts of his body simultaneously
   - Bottom only

3. Ask Matthew to show you his own ways of moving the paper plate across the room without using his hands.

Ways to Make It More Challenging

■ Give Matthew a visual target to look at as he moves across the room.

■ Make a path with tape for him to follow.

■ Place some obstacles in his way so that he has to maneuver around them.

What to Look For

■ Matthew keeps his hands away from the paper plate.

■ He positions his body to use the combinations requested.

■ He uses the correct body parts as requested.

MAKE-A-BALL

Making something and then watching it grow is satisfying. Like a seed you plant that turns into a flower, the Make-a-Ball will grow from a few rubber bands to be as big as your child wants it to be. You'll all have a ball!

Helps Your Child Develop and Enhance . . .
- Laterality (for wrapping your scarf around your neck)
- Motor planning (for wrapping presents and making a snowman)
- Proprioception (for making and throwing a snowball)
- Tactile processing (for reacting appropriately to the discomfort of cold snow in your boots and scarf)

What You Need
- Ping-Pong or golf ball
- Assortment of rubber bands

What You Do
1. Wrap four or five rubber bands around the ball to get it started.
2. Give Shelly a rubber band and ask her to wrap it around the ball.
3. Once she is successful, let her choose the rubber bands. Encourage her to wrap at least five bands around the ball at each sitting.

Ways to Make It More Challenging
- Have Shelly grow her Make-a-Ball with her eyes closed.
- Have her select specific rubber bands. For example, ask her to put on "three blue," or "two green and one orange," or "one thick and two skinny" rubber bands.
- Have Shelly bounce and catch the ball.
- Bounce the Make-a-Ball to Shelly for her to catch.

What to Look For

- Shelly uses both hands efficiently to wrap rubber bands as the ball grows in size. The challenge will change as the ball changes.
- She enjoys the challenge!

NEWSPAPER CRUMPLE

This is a fun way to make use of those old newspapers that are waiting to be recycled. Throwing the newspaper balls at each other at the end is especially fun. (Be aware that little hands tend to get dirty from the ink.)

Helps Your Child Develop and Enhance . . .
- Bilateral coordination (for doing push-ups and jumping jacks)
- Laterality (for propelling a scooter)
- Proprioception (for squeezing finger paint out of the tube)
- Tactile processing (for playing with stickers and finger paint)

What You Need
- Old newspaper pages
- Optional: laundry basket

What You Do
1. Give Betty a page of newspaper and ask, "Can you tear a big strip of paper from the top to the bottom?"
   - If necessary, show Betty how to tear a strip by starting at the top and tearing down to the bottom of the page. The strip should be about the size of a newspaper column.
   - If the newspaper page is too long for her, tear it in half width-wise and give her only half a sheet.
   - If she is unable to tear the paper, give her the paper already torn.
2. Say, "Show me how you can crumple this paper into a tiny little ball using just one hand." Betty will probably hold the paper against her body or put it on a surface to make it easier.

3. Say, "Squeeze the ball as tightly as you can so that it's very little."
4. Encourage Betty to throw her newspaper ball into a laundry basket.

Ways to Make It More Challenging
- Ask Betty to crumple a strip of newspaper in each hand *at the same time.*
- Ask her to race her hands, one against the other.

What to Look For
- Betty eventually crumples the paper using her hand *without* holding it against her body.
- She makes the ball as small as possible.

NOSE TO KNEE

Like yoga, Nose to Knee is a calming, centering, lengthening, and strengthening activity.

Helps Your Child Develop and Enhance . . .
- Balance (for walking through a pile of leaves)
- Body awareness (for hiding in a pile of leaves)
- Laterality (for holding a bag and stuffing it with leaves)
- Motor planning (for pretending to be a falling leaf)
- Proprioception (for raking and hauling a sack of leaves to the curb)
- Vestibular processing (for jumping into a leaf pile)

What You Need
- Mat or comfortable surface
- Optional: metronome

What You Do
1. Ask Mark to get on his hands and knees on the mat. Say, "Make your body look like a table. Be sure your back is flat." You may need to demonstrate the position.
2. Say, "Now round your back and very slowly bring your nose and knee together." Don't worry if Mark is unable to touch his nose to his knee. The important movement is the curling.

3. Say, "Now move that leg back and make it into a straight line behind you. Keep your knee off the mat. At the same time, bring your head up and look at the ceiling. Be sure your hands and other knee stay right where they are!"
4. Say, "Now put your knee down and make your body look like a table again."
5. Ask Mark to repeat the exercise with the other knee.
6. Have him repeat the entire sequence five times.

Ways to Make It More Challenging

- Mark makes his movements to a steady count, perhaps using a metronome.
- He holds each extension and flexion for a count of five.

What to Look For

- Mark holds his body still, other than his head and the knee he is moving.
- He is able to stay on his hands and one knee without sinking onto his elbows.
- He rounds his back smoothly and evenly as he brings his knee toward his nose.
- Mark is able to maintain his balance.
- He is able to switch sides without verbal or tactile cues.
- He moves *slowly*.

PAPER PLATE PLAY

This versatile activity can go wherever you find a smooth floor, including the kitchen, the classroom, or the all-purpose room at school. It is different from Look Ma, No Hands! (page 128) as it focuses on your child's feet. This activity, too, can be done alone or with a buddy. Your child will find many ways to vary it as he gets In Sync with the idea.

Helps Your Child Develop and Enhance . . .
- Laterality (for putting hair into a ponytail)
- Motor planning (for coordinating eyes and hands for writing and drawing)
- Proprioception (for playing Tug-of-War)

What You Need
- Two paper plates
- A smooth floor, such as a flat carpet or a hardwood or linoleum floor
- Optional: Masking tape, obstacles (for example, book, basket, toy), and metronome

What You Do
1. Give Jimmy one paper plate. Say, "Show me how you can move across the room with one foot on the plate and the other foot on the floor."
2. Say, "Switch feet, so your other foot is on the plate, and move back to where you started."
3. Give Jimmy the second plate. Say, "Now put one foot on each plate. Move across the room."

Ways to Make It More Challenging
- Give Jimmy a visual target to look at as he moves across the room.
- Make a path with masking tape for Jimmy to follow.

- Place some obstacles in his way so that he has to maneuver around them.
- Have him move his feet to the slow beat of a metronome.

What to Look For

- Jimmy keeps his feet on the plate(s).
- He swings his arms in a relaxed way as he slides across the room.

PENNY PASS

Penny Pass is an amazingly simple and simply amazing activity to promote visual attention and the all-important midline-crossing skill.
You can offer this activity anywhere and anytime you have a penny in
your pocket and a bit of time to fill. Try it at the kitchen table, or while
waiting for the waitress to bring the pancakes.

Helps Your Child Develop and Enhance . . .
- Directionality (drawing a five-point star and an asterisk)
- Midline crossing (for reading smoothly across the page)
- Visual tracking (for observing a falling leaf or a snowflake)

What You Need
- Penny or other coin
- Two chairs
- Optional: metronome

What You Do
1. Sit in a chair opposite Thom and show him a penny in your
   right hand.
2. Say, "Thom, watch my hand." Pass the penny from your right
   hand to your left hand, working slightly below Thom's eye level.
   Remind him: "Don't move your head, just move your eyes."

3. Say, "Thom, keep watching my hand." Then pass the penny from your left hand across to Thom's left hand.
4. Say, "Now just move the hand holding the penny and put the penny in your right (or "your other") hand."
5. Say, "Now pass the penny to me." Hold out your right hand. Thom will cross the midline to pass the penny from his right hand to your right hand.
6. Repeat Steps 2 through 5, starting with your left hand.

Ways to Make It More Challenging

- Use fewer and fewer verbal cues.
- Set a metronome to 40 beats per minute. Make each movement match the metronome's beat.

What to Look For

- Thom sits up straight, with his feet planted firmly on the floor (on a pile of phone books, if necessary).
- He moves his eyes only, not his head, in order to watch the penny. You can place a beanbag on Thom's head to minimize head movement.
- He crosses the midline by keeping his receiving hand in place.

WHEN YOU ARE facing Hugh to demonstrate an activity, his right hand will be opposite your left hand. If you want Hugh to start with his right hand, remember to start with your left.

PIPE CLEANER POKE

Pipe Cleaner Poke is a pleasant two-person activity that everyone enjoys. It is especially good for strengthening the visual system.

Helps Your Child Develop and Enhance . . .

- Laterality (for dribbling a basketball and galloping)
- Midline crossing (for playing Twister or T-ball)
- Spatial awareness (for understanding fractions and other math concepts)
- Visual processing (for putting coins into a piggy bank and pouring juice)

What You Need

- Three pipe cleaners in different colors, for example, yellow, red, and blue
- Optional: metronome

What You Do

1. Twist the yellow pipe cleaner so that there is a circle at the top.
2. Stand in front of Doris. Hold the yellow pipe cleaner in front of her. Give her the red pipe cleaner. Say, "Show me how you poke your pipe cleaner into my circle and back out again very quickly. Keep your pipe cleaner in the center of the circle so it doesn't touch."

3. Hold the yellow pipe cleaner in different positions (planes)—vertically, horizontally, high, low, and so forth—so that Doris has to shift where and how she moves her pipe cleaner.

4. Once Doris is successful with the red pipe cleaner, give her the blue one for her other hand. Say, "Now let's do this another way. This time, alternate your hands. First, poke your red pipe cleaner in and out." Move the yellow pipe cleaner so that Doris is crossing the midline in order to be successful. Say, "Now poke the blue one."

Ways to Make It More Challenging

- In Step 4, Doris alternates hands without your verbal cues.
- Doris pokes her fingers instead of pipe cleaners. Say, "Right, left," instead of "red" and "blue."
- She pokes her pipe cleaners in a pattern you call out, such as: "Right, right, left, right, right, left," or "Red, blue, both, red, blue, both."
- Add a metronome, starting with forty beats per minute.

What to Look For

- Doris is accurate when poking the pipe cleaners in the circle.
- She is equally successful in each plane.
- She holds her body straight while crossing the midline.

REACH FOR THE SKY

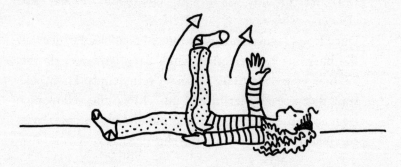

For kids and adults alike, stretching can be energizing and calming. Try this feel-good activity with your child first thing in the morning, at bedtime, or both. Remember to do it very slowly to get maximum benefit from a lovely, total body stretch.

Helps Your Child Develop and Enhance . . .
- Bilateral coordination (for playing the accordion)
- Body awareness (for putting on a sweater)
- Laterality (for using a fork)
- Motor planning (for playing Hide-and-Seek)
- Proprioception (for climbing a tree)

What You Need
- Mat or firm mattress
- Optional: metronome

What You Do
1. Have Karen lie on her back. Say, "Karen, stretch just one arm straight up to the sky. Keep your other arm down." (You may need to touch the limb you are asking her to stretch.)
2. Say, "Pretend you are melting. Bring your arm down. Let everything relax."
3. Say, "Now stretch your other arm and reach for the sky."

4. Repeat, in this order:
   - Single leg
   - Arms together
   - Legs together
   - Arm and leg on same side of her body
   - Arm and leg on opposite sides of her body

Ways to Make It More Challenging
- Karen holds each extension to the count of five.
- Karen makes the movements to the beat of a metronome.

What to Look For
- Karen stretches only the part(s) of her body called for.
- Her extended limbs are perpendicular to her body.
- Karen appears more focused after reaching for the sky.

ROLLING LOG

Rolling Log is an all-purpose activity—it provides great sensory stimulation through the whole body. If your kid loves to roll, this is a great activity. If your kid does not love to roll, give it a try anyway.

Helps Your Child Develop and Enhance . . .
- Directionality (for knowing which way to run after hitting the baseball)
- Motor planning (for sliding into home plate)
- Spatial awareness (for running to first base)
- Vestibular processing (for running backward to catch a fly ball)

What You Need
- Two different-colored beanbags

What You Do
1. Place Beanbag A on the floor as a marker and ask Jeremy to stand on it.
2. Hand Jeremy the other beanbag and say, "Throw Beanbag B anywhere on the floor." The distance should be 10 feet or less.

3. Say, "Lie on the floor and put your head on Beanbag A. Stretch out as straight as a log."
4. Point to Beanbag B and say, "Look over there at Beanbag B. Keep looking at it the whole time and roll toward it."
5. Say, "Stop with your head on Beanbag B. Great!"
6. Say, "Now stand on Beanbag B. Here, take Beanbag A, so you can do it again."

Ways to Make It More Challenging
- After Jeremy starts rolling, change the position of the beanbag, requiring him to alter his roll.
- Have him roll so that his knees, rather than his head, land on the beanbag.

What to Look For
- Jeremy rolls toward the beanbag continuously, without taking breaks for adjustment of direction.
- He throws the beanbag a little farther each time.
- He is able to make an adaptive response to change direction smoothly, midroll.
- He keeps his body as straight as a log.

ROUNDABOUT

Roundabout is a *slow* activity. It is similar to Chalkboard Circle (page 108) and easier and more appropriate for young children. Like Chalkboard Circle, Roundabout provides a great workout for the eyes. The ability to move one's eyes freely and precisely, with an economy of head motion, is an important survival skill—and academic skill and sports skill, as well. This activity makes the eye exercise amusing.

Helps Your Child Develop and Enhance . . .
- Midline crossing (for reading and sports)
- Motor planning (for writing and fine motor skills)
- Visual tracking (for scanning a shelf to find a book)

What You Need
- Chalkboard or a large piece of paper or poster board on the wall
- Chalk or crayon
- Small car, such as a Matchbox car
- Optional: beanbag

What You Do
1. On a large chalkboard, draw a roundabout (a large circle of double lines about 6 inches apart) at Benjy's eye level. At the top of the circle, draw a line connecting the inner and outer lines, to be the starting line.
2. Give Benjy a small car and say, "Stand tall here at the chalkboard and show me how *slowly* you can drive your car around the roundabout. Be sure to keep it on the road."
3. Say, "Watch the car as you move it along. Keep your head as still as you can." Remind: "Just your eyes and hand move," or challenge: "Don't let anyone see you move your head!" To help Benjy hold his head still, put a beanbag on his head.

4. Say, "Go around five times. Then go five times in the other direction."
5. Say, "Wonderful! Your driver saw everything all around him. Now put the car in your other hand and do it again."

Ways to Make It More Challenging

- Draw a new, narrower roundabout.
- Have Benjy do this exercise while balancing on a balance board.
- Make the road in the shape of an infinity sign.

What to Look For

- Benjy stands tall.
- He moves his arm freely and holds his head still.
- He holds the car in the same hand throughout (do not let him switch hands at the midline).
- He uses slow, smooth movements.

SHAPE RAIN

Cutting out the shapes takes a lot of work up front, but your child's giggles will make your preparations worth the effort. You may want to laminate the paper or poster board *before* cutting out the shapes to make them last longer. Shape Rain is great for one child or for a group, especially because everyone can succeed regardless of developmental stage.

Helps Your Child Develop and Enhance . . .
- Bilateral coordination (for working out with barbells)
- Body awareness (for doing the Hokey Pokey)
- Motor planning (for smooth, efficient movement)
- Vestibular processing (for doing gymnastics)
- Visual processing (for finding your friend in a crowded room)

What You Need
- Squares, circles, triangles, and rectangles cut from red, blue, yellow, and green construction paper (a total of 40 to 50 shapes)
- Music
- Room to move

What You Do
1. Hold up a blue triangle and ask, "Sasha, what shape is this? What color is it?" Do the same with each shape and color.
2. Toss an assortment of the shapes (about half) into the air and watch them fall slowly to the ground. Toss them so that they spread over a fairly large area.
3. Put on some music. Say, "Sasha, when the music starts, jump on both feet all around the room. When the music stops, put your nose on a red square." Other ideas for directions include:
   - Creep on hands and knees. Stop and stand on a blue shape.
   - Slither like a snake. Stop and sit on a circle.

- Tiptoe. Stop and put your pointer fingers on a yellow triangle.
- Roll across the floor. Stop and put your chin on a red rectangle.
- Walk backward slowly. Stop and put your head on a green square.

4. To clean up, say, "Sasha, when the music starts, bring me all the red circles." Other cleanup ideas include:
   - All the blue shapes
   - One triangle and two green shapes
   - Three shapes that are different
   - As many shapes as your age
   - As many shapes as there are letters in your name

Ways to Make It More Challenging

- Increase the number of shapes.
- Increase the complexity of directions:
  - Put your nose on a red circle and your elbow on something blue.
  - Put one foot on a triangle and one foot on a square.
  - Put your chin on a square and each hand on a differently colored shape.

What to Look For

- Sasha uses the body part(s) requested.
- She follows directions accurately.

SHOULDER SHRUG

Many of us hold our tension in our shoulders. Shoulder Shrug is a fun way to relieve *your* tension while helping your child gain a better understanding of his body. The activity also improves posture and readies the arms for more involved tasks such as handwriting.

Helps Your Child Develop and Enhance . . .
- Bilateral coordination (for holding a kite string with both hands)
- Body awareness (for putting your sneakers on the correct feet)
- Directionality (for knowing which way to run to keep the kite aloft)
- Laterality (for pulling in the kite string, hand over hand)
- Proprioception (for holding a kite string on a windy day)

What You Need
- Pair of shoulders
- Optional: metronome

What You Do
1. Say, "Jacob, watch me," as you shrug your shoulders up and down. "Can you shrug your shoulders like me?" If Jacob has difficulty moving his shoulders, press your hand against his shoulder in the direction opposite to the way you ask him to move it. In other words, if he has difficulty shrugging a shoulder *up*, press your hand *down* on that shoulder and say, "Push against my hand."
2. Ask Jacob if he can:
   - Shrug one shoulder at a time.
   - Shrug one shoulder up and one shoulder down at the same time.

- Move one shoulder forward.
- Move both shoulders back at the same time.
- Move one shoulder forward and the other shoulder back.

3. Say, "Jacob, show me your own special way of moving your shoulders."

Ways to Make It More Challenging

- Have Jacob sit on a ball or stand on a balance board while shrugging his shoulders.
- Have him shrug his shoulders in a pattern you make up together, such as forward, forward, up, down.
- Have him move his shoulders to the beat of a metronome.

What to Look For

- Jacob can isolate each shoulder from the rest of his body.
- He moves only the shoulder called for.

SINGING STRING

Take a 3-foot length of fishing line, a flat piece of wood, a lacing bead—put them together and presto—you've got the quintessential string bass! Carol thinks this activity is the cat's meow. It encourages kids to listen carefully to the high and low sounds they can produce at will by altering the tension of the string. To make this experience more accessible to a young child or a child with motor coordination difficulties, tie the end of the fishing line to a doorknob instead of asking him to stabilize it with his foot.

Helps Your Child Develop and Enhance . . .

- Balance (for staying upright in a canoe)
- Laterality (for reeling in the fish)
- Midline crossing (for paddling a canoe)
- Motor planning (for getting yourself out of the canoe)
- Proprioception (for casting a fishing line)
- Tactile processing (for placing the bait on the hook)

What You Need

- 3-foot length of 30-pound fishing line
- Flat piece of wood, about 8 inches long
- Lacing bead or wooden ring

What You Do

1. To prepare the Singing String, have Jamal help you tie one end of the fishing line around the center of the wood. Attach the bead (as a handle) to the loose end of the string.
2. Say, "Jamal, step on the wood and hold the bead in one hand. Now pull the bead until the string is taut, and pluck it with your other hand." If necessary, demonstrate how to use your index finger to pull and release the string.
3. Say, "Now pull the bead to tighten the string even more. Pluck it. Is the sound higher or lower than before?" (Higher, because a tight string makes fast vibrations, and fast vibrations have a high pitch.)
4. Say, "Let's hum that sound."
5. Say, "Relax the tension on the string just a bit, and now pluck it. How does the string sound now?" (Lower, because a loose string makes slow vibrations.) "Let's hum the low sound."
6. Have Jamal switch hands to hold and pluck the string.

Ways to Make It More Challenging

- Have Jamal stretch the string off to his sides so he must reach across his body to make the string "sing."
- Have him make up a conversation between a child and parent, or elephant and mouse, as he changes the tension and thus the sound on the string.
- Together, sing Jamal's favorite song while he "accompanies" it by twanging on the Singing String.

What to Look For

- Jamal can maintain his balance while he stabilizes the piece of wood with his foot, stretches the string with one hand, and plucks the string with the other hand.
- He stretches and holds the string taut enough to produce sound.

TAP ME SILLY

Your child set the table without being asked? Tied both shoelaces? Passed the math facts quiz? Found the missing mitten? Hooray! Celebrate every achievement! Kids learn this cheerful activity quickly and enjoy repeating it five, ten, fifteen times a day. You, too, will value using Tap Me Silly as a reward, not only because it is simple and fun, but also because it reinforces all the important skills listed below.

Helps Your Child Develop and Enhance . . .
- Balance (for standing on one foot)
- Laterality (for stretching your bubblegum)
- Midline crossing (for putting on a Band-Aid)
- Motor planning (for getting in and out of the sandbox)

What You Need
- Enthusiasm

What You Do
1. Stand facing Jesse and say, "Let's tap and spell S-I-L-L-Y."
2. Hold up your right hand and say, "Tap me 'S'!" Be sure Jesse taps your hand with his right hand.

3. Now hold your left hand up and say, "Tap me 'I'!" Be sure Jesse uses his left hand.
4. Bend forward and hold your right hand in front of Jesse's legs, at his midline. Say, "Tap me 'L'!" Be sure Jesse taps your hand with his right foot.
5. Continue with your left hand and Jesse's left foot. "Tap me another 'L'!"
6. Hold up your hands, thumbs together, palms facing Jesse. Say, "Tap me 'Y'! Tap my hands with your head."

Ways to Make It More Challenging
- Count, "One, two, three . . ." rather than spelling "S-I-L-L-Y."
- Count by threes or fours.
- Spell names or other words, adding different body parts as needed.

What to Look For
- Jesse uses his appropriate limb to tap your hands.
- He makes contact with his hands and feet accurately.
- He maintains his balance throughout the activity.

REMEMBER THE RHYMES you chanted while bouncing a ball, jumping rope, or playing hand games? Remember "Take Me Out to the Ball Game," "Miss Mary Mack," and "A, My Name Is Alice"? These old-fashioned games are better than any computer game for developing and enhancing many of the skills children need—and emphasize all the skills we have covered in this book. Sometimes our parents knew what they were talking about without even realizing it when they said, "Go outside and play!"

TUMMY ON THE BALL

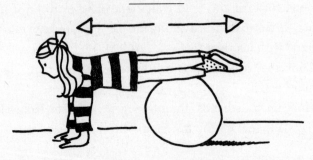

The equipment for this activity is a ball that is big enough for your child to sit on comfortably, with feet squarely on the floor. This activity is just what you need to improve balance, posture, and strength. For older kids, you may want to use a therapy ball, sometimes called a stability ball. While stability seems elusive at first, your child will get the hang of it after a bit of practice.

Helps Your Child Develop and Enhance . . .
- Balance (for riding a scooter)
- Motor planning (for pouring a drink from a thermos)
- Proprioception (for carrying a picnic basket)
- Vestibular processing (for sitting at a picnic table)

What You Need
- Therapy ball, sized so that when the child sits on it, her knees are at right angles and her feet rest squarely on the floor.
- Padded surface, such as gym mat, carpet, or grass.

What You Do
1. Ask Michelle to stand behind the ball. Say, "Put your tummy on the ball and your hands on the floor."
2. Say, "Walk your hands forward so your legs are resting on the ball. Keep your body as stiff as a board. Stay on the ball! Go as far forward as you can and then stop."
3. Say, "Now move backward so your tummy is on the ball where it started."

Ways to Make It More Challenging

- Michelle walks her hands farther away each time so that first her thighs, then her knees, and finally her ankles rest on top of the ball.
- She holds the far position for at least 10 seconds.

What to Look For

- Michelle's body remains on the ball throughout the exercise.
- Her body stays parallel to the floor without twisting.
- Her arms stay extended. No landing on elbows!

TWEEZE AND SPELL

This activity is a fun way to practice spelling words, or to make gifts for friends.

Helps Your Child Develop and Enhance . . .
- Midline crossing (for waving a flag from side to side and giving yourself a hug)
- Proprioception (for tweezing eyebrows and taking out splinters)
- Tactile processing (for buttoning and zipping)

What You Need
- Alphabet noodles
- Dark construction paper
- Tweezers
- Glue

What You Do
1. Sit on the right side of Hailey.
2. Place a piece of paper in front of her and spread out some alphabet noodles on it.
3. Give Hailey a tweezers and ask, "Can you pick up the letters in your name? Put them in my hand." Help Hailey locate the letters if she's having trouble.
4. Start with the letters in front of her. Gradually, move the paper with the letters on it to the left side of the table if she is right-handed, or to the right if she is left-handed, so that Hailey has to reach across her midline to pick up each letter.
5. Introduce a second piece of paper and place it in front of her. This is where she will now put the letters.

Ways to Make It More Challenging

- Hailey spells words from her spelling homework using the alphabet noodles.
- She glues the letters onto ice cream sticks or buttons to make pins as gifts.
- She places the noodles on lines that you have previously drawn onto paper.

What to Look For

- Hailey holds the tweezers between her thumb and her pointer finger.
- She keeps the tweezers in her working hand without switching hands.
- She moves her arm freely across her midline rather than turning her body.

WHEN PAUL COLORS or does his homework at the kitchen table, be sure that the chair and table are at the proper height. His ankles, knees, and elbows should be at right angles. His feet should rest flat on the floor, a stool, or a telephone book, and his lower arm from the elbow down should rest comfortably on the table or desk as he writes.

WAKE UP, ARMS!

Throwing a ball, writing your name, and hugging your best friend all require arm strength. This activity helps awaken the arms and improves core strength, as well.

Helps Your Child Develop and Enhance . . .
- Directionality (for playing miniature golf)
- Motor planning (for climbing over a wall)
- Proprioception (for slicing carrots)

What You Need
- A chair low enough for David to place his feet flat on the floor (or on a telephone book, if necessary)

What You Do
1. Have David sit in the chair with his feet flat on the floor. Stand in front of him. Say, "Raise one arm straight up in the air. I am going to push your arm back. Your job is to resist with all your might. Push *just* your arm against my hand."
2. Put your hand on his forearm and exert pressure to push his arm back.
3. Now stand behind David, and repeat the exercise:
   - You press his arm forward, while he pushes his arm back.
   - You press his arm to the right, while he pushes his arm to the left.
   - You press his arm to the left, while he pushes his arm to the right.
   - You press his other arm in four directions, while he resists.

Ways to Make It More Challenging
- Have David hold the resistance in each direction for a count of three to five.
- David pushes your arm.

What to Look For

- David uses only his arm to resist, *not* his entire body.
- David keeps his arm extended throughout the activity.
- He resists in the correct direction.
- He stays squarely seated in his chair without contorting his body in order to resist.

WALK THE PLANK

How does a sixteen-year-old learn to drive? By moving through space, over and over again, for about sixteen years! Driving lessons begin early, as the developing child learns to run across a busy playground, dribble a ball toward the goal, and weave through a crowded school corridor. Before navigating a car, *of course*, kids must practice navigating their bodies through a variety of pathways.

Helps Your Child Develop and Enhance . . .
- Balance (for climbing stairs)
- Directionality (for reeling in a kite string)
- Motor planning (for climbing into a treehouse)
- Vestibular processing (for riding a bicycle over a bumpy path)
- Visual processing (for lining up numbers in a math problem or words on a page)

What You Need
- Masking tape
- Optional: Beanbags, blocks, or balloon

What You Do
1. Place two long strips of masking tape on the floor, about 12 inches apart.
2. Say, "Eden, can you walk the plank between the lines? Remember to stay inside the lines."
3. Have Eden navigate the path in different ways:
   - Backward
   - Sideways, left foot leading
   - Sideways, right foot leading
   - Marching
   - Jumping
   - Hopping

Ways to Make It More Challenging

- Weekly, replace the tape, gradually decreasing the space between the lines, so that in the end, Eden will be balancing on a single line. Take as much time as she needs to get there.
- Place small obstacles, such as beanbags or blocks, for Eden to avoid while navigating the plank.
- Ask Eden to tap a balloon with her hands to keep it in the air while she walks the plank.
- Make the plank curvy.

What to Look For

- Eden stays within the lines.
- She is able to move as requested in the proper direction.

WATCH YOUR HANDS CREEP

Creeping on all fours is an essential developmental activity. (Often this is refered to as crawling, which is, in fact, moving on one's belly with the help of one's arms and legs.) Creeping (and crawling) is important for getting the two sides of the body in sync, for building strength in the muscles and bones, for reading and writing, for catching a ball, for riding a bike, for . . . you name it!

Helps Your Child Develop and Enhance . . .
- Laterality (for establishing handedness)
- Motor planning (for square dancing)
- Tactile processing (for washing your hands and face)
- Visual processing (for eye-body coordination and doing crossword puzzles)

What You Need
- Room to move in a straight line
- Masking tape
- Optional: metronome

What You Do
1. Say, "Harry, get on your hands and knees. Show me how you can creep around the room."
2. Place two parallel lines of masking tape (about 12 inches apart) on the floor. Say, "Harry, slide your hands on the tape as you creep from here to there. Be sure to watch your hands as you slide them."

Ways to Make It More Challenging
- Ask Harry to say "right" or "left" as he looks at his hand.
- Ask him to creep to the beat of a metronome.

What to Look For

- Harry creeps in a contralateral fashion (moving hand and knee on opposite sides of his body).
- He is able to slide his hands along the tape, while looking at them.
- He is able to move his hands and his knees in a coordinated fashion.

Advanced Activities

▼

CLOCK WISE

Remember using an analog clock to learn to tell time? Remember mastering terms such as clockwise, counterclockwise, a quarter to four, half past seven . . . ? Digital timepieces—like Velcro shoelaces, automatic doors, and "magic" faucets that require you to do nothing except be there—mean that our children have fewer opportunities to learn essential self-help skills. Learning to read an analog clock is an important life skill that does much more than teach a child to tell time.

Helps Your Child Develop and Enhance . . .
- Bilateral coordination (for tying shoelaces)
- Directionality (for understanding "clockwise" and "counterclockwise")
- Laterality (for turning on a faucet and brushing one's hair)
- Midline crossing (for playing miniature golf)
- Motor planning (for playing on playground equipment)
- Spatial awareness (for understanding fractions and other math concepts)

What You Need

- Analog clock—the bigger, the better
- Chalkboard and chalk, or easel and crayon
- Sticker to identify your child's "minute hand"

What You Do

1. Show Savanna an analog clock. Point out where the numbers lie on the clock face: 12 is at the top, 6 is at the bottom, 3 is on the right, and 9 is on the left.
2. Ask her to draw a huge circle on the board. This will be her clock.
3. Ask her to put the numbers 12, 6, 3, and 9 in their appropriate places on her clock face.
4. Put the sticker on her left hand. Say, "This is the minute hand. Your other hand is the hour hand. Put your minute hand on the 12."
5. Say, "Now show me where your hour hand goes if it's 3 o'clock."
6. Ask Savanna to show you other times using the four numbers:
   - Noon (both hands on 12)
   - Quarter past 3 (both hands on 3)
   - 6 o'clock (left hand on 12, right hand on 6)
   - 9:30 (right hand on 9, left hand on 6)

Ways to Make It More Challenging

- Have Savanna fill in the remaining numbers on her clock. Have her point to the numbers, starting on 1 and bouncing her finger clockwise from 1 to 12 as she names the numbers. Have her bounce her finger again as she recites, "5, 10, 15, 20 . . . 55, 60." Now play Clock Wise again, using all the clock numbers.
- With your finger, draw a circle on Savanna's back. Press your finger where 12 would be and ask, "What number is this?" Repeat for 6, 3, and 9.
- Ask her to identify the remaining clock numbers as you press their locations on her back. (You may need to keep a finger on the imaginary 12 or 6 as a reference.)

What to Look For

- Savanna consistently uses her left hand as the minute hand and her right hand as the hour hand.
- She places her hands on the numbers accurately.

FOLLOW THE BUG

When children keep their eyes fixed on a TV or computer screen, they deny themselves the opportunity to develop adequate visual tracking. We use visual tracking to read words across a page, play kickball, and perceive oncoming cars before merging into a lane of traffic. Before you ask your child to Follow the Bug, try this activity yourself. You will see that once you are able to Follow the Bug without the help of a flashlight, you can take the activity anywhere.

Helps Your Child Develop and Enhance . . .
- Bilateral coordination (for hugging another person)
- Midline crossing (for hugging oneself)
- Motor planning (for hula hooping)
- Visual tracking (for swatting a fly)

What You Need
- Wall in a dimly lit room
- Flashlight
- Chair

What You Do
1. Have Sophie sit in an appropriately sized chair, that is, one that allows her feet to rest comfortably on the floor.
2. Say, "Sophie, hold this flashlight with both hands. Pretend that a bug is crawling along the line where the wall meets the ceiling. Shine your light on the make-believe bug."
3. Say, "Pretend the bug is creeping very slowly along the line, from left to right. Keep your light right on it! Keep your head still and use just your eyes."

Ways to Make It More Challenging

- Sophie follows the imaginary bug's path from top to bottom along the seam where two walls meet.
- Sophie follows the bug around the perimeter of one wall, moving the flashlight left to right, top to bottom, right to left, and bottom to top. Reverse direction.
- She follows the bug with her eyes without the help of a flashlight.

What to Look For

- Sophie holds the flashlight with both hands at all times.
- She moves the flashlight very slowly.
- Her head movement is minimal.

HOW MANY STEPS?

This is a terrific exercise to do with a visual target such as a beanbag, when you are housebound and needing a movement break. The activity is just as effective when you're walking to the car or when you're at the playground. Just use objects you see, such as a tree or a house, rather than a beanbag as your target.

Helps Your Child Develop and Enhance . . .
- Body awareness (for sports and ease of movement)
- Directionality (for handwriting and math)
- Motor planning (for negotiating an obstacle course)
- Spatial awareness (for following a "treasure map")

What You Need
- Two items, such as beanbags, washcloths, coins, or pebbles, to use as markers—one for a starting place and one for a target
- Space to move

What You Do
1. Put one beanbag on the floor and ask Aisha to stand on it.
2. Hand her the second beanbag and say, "Toss this beanbag in any direction."
3. Say, "The game is to estimate (or "to guess") how many steps it will take for you to walk to the beanbag. Make your steps the same size. Think about it and tell me: How many steps?"
4. After Aisha gives an estimate, do not disagree or laugh, even if it is way off. Say, "Okay. Walk to the beanbag. Look at it the whole time you're moving toward it. Let's count your steps together."
5. If her estimate is correct, have her throw the beanbag from that spot in another direction and repeat the activity.
6. If Aisha is inaccurate, ask her to come back to her starting place. Place a marker on the ground, half the distance between Aisha and the beanbag. Ask her to estimate again to the closer target.

Ways to Make It More Challenging

- Ask Aisha to take her steps to the beat of a metronome.
- Ask her to jump or march instead of walking to the beanbag.
- Ask her to move through space for longer distances.
- Suggest the number of steps she should take to reach her target. Now she will need to adjust her gait to measure out baby steps or giant steps.

What to Look For

- Aisha's steps are equal and normal size (no baby steps, no giant steps, except when requested).
- Aisha looks at the target the whole time she is moving.
- Aisha is accurate in her counting. (If she is way off, you can help her assess her mistakes by saying things like, "Gee, your legs can stretch longer than you knew, so you needed fewer steps than you thought." If she underestimated, say, "Gosh, the beanbag is farther away than you thought. Maybe a really tall giant could get there in three steps, but a kid your size needs to take more than three.")

JUMPING ARROWS

Jumping is a feel-good-all-over activity. It provides important sensory input, "awakens" the body and brain, organizes a child's behavior, and improves attention and learning. Jumping Arrows can be done outdoors on a large trampoline or indoors on a minitrampoline. Safety is paramount, especially on a minitrampoline. If possible, use one that has a handle bar. If you are concerned that your child may fall off, bank the trampoline with pillows to ensure a soft landing.

Helps Your Child Develop and Enhance . . .
- Balance (for staying upright while moving)
- Bilateral coordination (for jumping rope and playing Cat's Cradle)
- Directionality (for turning faucets on and off)
- Motor planning (for climbing over a wall)
- Vestibular processing (for rolling and somersaulting)
- Visual tracking (for doing word-find activities)

What You Need
- Trampoline
- Chalkboard and chalk, or poster board and marker

What You Do
1. On the board, draw a row of about eight arrows, similar to this:

2. Place the minitrampoline in front of the board so Frannie can easily see the arrows. Say, "Frannie, start jumping. Now look at the arrows, starting with the first one on the line, and tell me which way they are pointing—up, down, right, or left."

3. Add one or two more rows of arrows pointing in different directions. Ask Frannie to read the entire chart aloud as she continues to jump. Add as many more rows as you like.

What to Look For

- Frannie accurately calls out the directions of the arrows.
- She jumps rhythmically and steadily.

Ways to Make It More Challenging

- Ask Frannie to call out the direction of the next arrow simultaneously with every other jump.
- Ask her to interlock her fingers and to use both hands together to point in the direction of each arrow as she says it.

MARVELOUS MARIONETTES

This activity is fun and funny. It's also challenging, so be sure to introduce it slowly. If it's too hard today, try it another time. Most kids will rise to the challenge.

Helps Your Child Develop and Enhance . . .

- Body awareness (for moving over and under obstacles)
- Laterality (for moving a toy train along its track)
- Motor planning (for setting up the train track)
- Proprioception (for pushing open a heavy door)

What You Need

- Metronome
- Stickers (or pieces of masking tape), numbered 1, 2, 3, and 4
- Visual target

What You Do

1. Put stickers on Robbie's arms and legs:
   - Left arm = 1
   - Right arm = 2
   - Left foot = 3
   - Right foot = 4

2. Say, "When I say, 'One,' move your left arm forward. When I say, 'Two,' drop your left arm and move your right arm forward. When I say, 'Three,' put your right arm down and step forward with your left foot. When I say, 'Four,' step forward with your right foot."

3. Say, "Remember to move your arm back to your side when you move your other arm or take a step."

4. Call out a number and watch Robbie move an arm or take a step.

5. When Robbie can move each limb easily, say, "Move across the room in this pattern":

- 1, 2, 3, 4
- 1, 3, 4, 2
- 2, 3, 4, 1
- 3, 4, 1, 2
- 1 and 3 together, 2 and 4 together
- 1 and 4 together, 2 and 3 together

Ways to Make It More Challenging

- Remove stickers so that Robbie has to commit the numbers and their corresponding movements to memory.
- Ask him to call out the number as he moves his arm or leg.
- Ask Robbie to make his movements to the *slow* beat of a metronome.
- Change the pattern while Robbie is partway across the room.
- Have him go backward.

What to Look For

- Robbie moves the correct limbs.
- He looks at the target.
- He moves *only* the limb called for and not others.
- He moves his arm and leg at the same time, when appropriate.

ROLL-A-PATH

In life, getting from Point A to Point B takes practice, whether the path is through an obstacle course, from the classroom to the cafeteria, or along the route of the Boston Marathon. Learning to maneuver your body to stick to the path is a skill worth mastering.

Helps Your Child Develop and Enhance . . .

- Body awareness (for dressing dolls and yourself)
- Directionality (for noticing differences in letters such as b and d, and p and q)
- Motor planning (for handwriting and hula hooping)
- Spatial awareness (for judging distances on paper and in space)
- Vestibular processing (for moving from one place to another)

What You Need

- Masking tape
- Enough room to roll across the floor

What You Do

1. Make a path with a single line of masking tape on the floor. Start with a straight path, longer than 8 feet, if possible.
2. Say, "Ralph, lie on the floor and put your head on the path, right at the start. Can you roll beside this path, keeping your head on the tape the whole time?" Initially, help him position himself so his body is perpendicular to the path.

3. Have Ralph roll several times in each direction.
4. Next, say, "Roll again, and this time keep your knees on the tape the whole time."
5. Have Ralph repeat the activity, rolling these body parts on the path:
   - Shoulders
   - Waist
   - Feet

Ways to Make It More Challenging
- Lay down a curved path.
- Lay down two parallel lines of tape (straight or curved), placed apart about the same distance as Ralph's height. Ask Ralph to roll *between the lines*.
- Gradually narrow the width of the path within which Ralph is expected to roll, so he is required to scrunch himself into a smaller and smaller ball.

What to Look For
- Ralph rolls in a *continuous* line, without stopping.
- He rolls his body as one unit, rather than leading with any one body part.
- He keeps the requested body part on the path.

TICK, TOCK, BODY CLOCK

This is a great game for a child who has already mastered telling time on an analog clock. Different from Clock Wise (page 169), Tick, Tock, Body Clock encourages your child to use his whole body to internalize the concept of telling time.

Helps Your Child Develop and Enhance . . .

- Bilateral coordination (for carrying a platter to the table)
- Directionality (for knowing which way to pass the platter)
- Laterality (for using a fork and knife to cut your food)
- Motor planning (for flipping pancakes)
- Spatial awareness (for arranging food on your plate)
- Proprioception (for reaching for the juice pitcher)

What You Need

- Chalk or stick to delineate a circle, or a circular throw rug
- Four beanbags or other markers

What You Do

1. Make a large circle on the ground with a radius of about 4 feet, or use a circular rug. This will be Brendan's clock.
2. Ask Brendan to put a beanbag on the spots where 12, 6, 3, and 9 would be.
3. Say, "Stand in the middle of the clock. Pretend your arm is the minute hand and your leg is the hour hand. Using your arm and leg, show me 9:30." (It's all right for Brendan to switch arms and legs to show different times, as long as one arm is the minute hand and one leg is the hour hand.)
4. Ask Brendan to show you different times, using 12, 3, 6, and 9, such as:
   - 6:00
   - 3:00
   - 6:15
   - 12:45

Ways to Make It More Challenging

- Add the other numbers to the clock. You can use beanbags, chalk, stickers, or whatever you have on hand to mark the numbers.
- Ask Brendan to use opposite arm and leg to tell the time.

What to Look For

- Brendan extends his minute hand and hour hand fully.
- He places his minute and hour hand on or close to the suggested "time."

WRITE THROUGH ME

Write Through Me, a variation of Back Drawing (page 99), also involves writing on your child's back and having him perceive what you have drawn. In the Write Through Me activity, however, the challenge is greater, as the child must draw a reproduction of your drawing as you "draw" it.

Helps Your Child Develop and Enhance . . .
- Directionality (for awareness of concepts such as up/down and left/right)
- Spatial awareness (for neat schoolwork)
- Tactile processing (for tying shoes and keyboarding)
- Visual processing (for drawing and writing accurately)

What You Need
- Chalkboard and chalk, or paper and pencil or crayon

What You Do
1. Ask Michael to sit on a chair with his back facing you.
2. Say, "I'm going to draw a design on your back. I want you to draw the same design on the chalkboard (or piece of paper)."

3. With your finger, draw a straight line (in any direction) on Michael's back. Have him chalk a line on the board moving in the same direction as your line on his back.
4. Draw a line going in a different direction on Michael's back and have him reproduce it on the board.

Ways to Make It More Challenging

- Begin your shapes in different places on Michael's back.
- Draw more complex designs and shapes for Michael to reproduce.

What to Look For

- Michael accurately reproduces the line, moving the chalk in the same direction as you moved your finger.
- He tolerates your drawing on his back.

ZANY NAME WALK

The ability to do more than one thing at a time becomes increasingly important as our lives become more complex. Zany Name Walk is a novel introduction to the everyday requirement of multitasking, necessary for playing sports, keeping on top of homework, and listening to music while doing chores.

Helps Your Child Develop and Enhance . . .
- Directionality (for making paper airplanes and origami swans)
- Motor planning (for sequencing and carrying out complex movements)

What You Need
- Space to walk

What You Do
1. Say, "Walk slowly across the room, saying the alphabet as you walk. Say one letter each time you take a step."
2. Say, "Do it again, and this time, when you say a letter in your name, clap your hands." For example, Caroline's pattern is: "A (clap), b, C (clap), d, E (clap), f, g, h, I (clap), j, k, L (clap), m, N (clap), O (clap), p, q, R (clap), s, t, u, v, w, x, y, z."

Ways to Make It More Challenging
- Caroline walks backward.
- She changes direction each time she says a letter in her name.
- She claps spelling words, her full name, or her address.
- She marches, tiptoes, or skips.

What to Look For
- Caroline recites the alphabet accurately.
- She coordinates her steps with her letters.
- She recognizes the letters in her name and claps appropriately.

PART FOUR

Appendices

▼

Watching Your Child Grow
Developmental Milestones

▼

A S YOU NOW know, children develop at different rates and at different times. Developmental norms are broad in range. Sammy may learn to walk at ten months and speak in sentences at the age of three; Amanda may learn to walk at eighteen months and speak coherently at a year. They are both meeting their milestones comfortably within the range of typical development.

Here are general guidelines for watching your child's sequential development in basic motor skills, beginning at age two. Remember that these are only guidelines and should not be used for diagnostic purposes. Should you have concerns, consult your pediatrician.

WALKING

When your child is between the ages of two and three, she will . . .
- Walk with less of a toddle.
- Walk without watching her feet.
- Make heel-toe contact with the floor, resulting in a smoother gait.
- Step over low obstacles.
- Have more flexibility at her knees and her ankles.
- Have more relaxed arms that move in coordination with her feet.
- Begin to swivel her hips.

When your child is between the ages of three and four, he will . . .
- Be able to walk on tiptoes.
- Be able to turn corners without elaborate preparation and precaution.
- No longer look or act as top heavy as before.
- Hold his shoulders more erect.
- Have well-established heel-toe foot movement.
- Be able to take walking and running steps on his toes.
- Swing his arms instead of using them for balance.

(He may go through a period of "uncoordination"—stumbling and falling—because he no longer pays attention to his movements as he did before.)

When your child is between the ages of four and five, she will . . .
- Walk steadily.
- Walk with long, swinging steps as adults do.

When your child is between the ages of five and six, he will . . .
- Take longer steps than before.
- Walk with ease, grace, and economy of movement.
- Be able to walk moderate distances on his toes.

RUNNING

When your child is between the ages of two and three, he . . .

- May fall down at the beginning of his run.
- May hold his hands up and forward.
- Will use his arms for balance.
- Will run while holding hands with another child.
- May fall down in the middle of his run.
- Will have more flexibility in his ankles, knees, and hips.
- Will have a smoother stride than before.
- Will run with greater speed than before.
- Will be learning to speed up and to slow down.

When your child is between the ages of three and four, she will . . .

- Run more smoothly than she did at two years.
- Have a more even stride than before.
- Regulate the speed of her run.
- Learn to turn sharp corners and to make sudden stops.
- Run forward easily and smoothly.

When your child is between the ages of four and five, he will . . .

- Enjoy more effective control over stopping, starting, and turning corners.
- Run efficiently with good form.
- Move his opposite arm and leg simultaneously.

When your child is between the ages of five and six, she will . . .

- Run smoothly.
- Run with increased speed.
- Use her running skills effectively in games.

JUMPING

When your child is between the ages of two and three, she will . . .

- Jump down from a bottom stair, one foot leading the other.
- Jump up off the floor, one foot leading the other.

When your child is between the ages of three and four, he will . . .

- Jump from the bottom stair, both feet together, without help.
- Jump down from a height of 18 to 24 inches, one foot leading the other, with help.
- Jump in place, with his feet together.
- Jump forward with both feet.
- Jump a distance of 14 to 24 inches on the ground.
- Jump over a rope held 6 inches off the floor with his feet together.

When your child is between the ages of four and five, she will . . .

- Crouch for a standing broad jump of 8 to 10 inches.
- Crouch for a high jump of 2 inches.
- Jump down from height of 18 to 24 inches with both feet together, without help.
- Do a running broad jump, showing fairly skillful jumping.

When your child is between the ages of five and six, he will . . .

- Be more adept at jumping over obstacles when running.
- Jump straight up higher than before.
- Jump forward farther than before.

BALANCING

When your child is between the ages of two and three, he will . . .
- Walk sideways and backward, although not in a straight line.
- Fall down less frequently when walking and running.
- Attempt to stand on one foot (thirty months).

When your child is between the ages of three and four, she will . . .
- Stand on one foot for two to five seconds.
- Maintain her equilibrium with her heels together when standing.
- Rise from a squatting position without help.
- Balance momentarily on her toes.
- Walk on a 10-foot path of 1-inch masking tape without stepping off.
- Walk on a 10-foot path of 1-inch masking tape, heel-to-toe.
- Walk backward in a straight line.

When your child is between the ages of four and five, he will . . .
- Walk on a 4-inch-wide balance beam alternating his feet.
- Show good balance when kicking.
- Maintain his balance for four to eight seconds on one foot.
- Walk a circular path (1 inch wide, 4 feet in diameter) without stepping off.
- Walk on a 2- to 3-inch board, alternating feet, partway before stepping off.

When your child is between the ages of five and six, she will . . .
- Balance on her toes for several seconds.
- Stand on one foot for over 10 seconds.

HOPPING, SKIPPING, GALLOPING

Hopping on two feet involves landing on the balls of the feet, as opposed to jumping in place, which involves landing on the balls of the feet and then onto the heel as well.

When your child is between the ages of two and three, she will . . .
- Be unable to stand momentarily on one foot.
- Attempt to hop while looking at her feet.
- Gallop while running. (She may run in the form of a gallop, but she will be unable to gallop on command.)
- Take short running steps on her toes.

When your child is between the ages of three and four, he will . . .
- Stand on one foot with momentary balance.
- "Hop" with an irregular series of jumps on both feet.
- Hop from two to three steps on both feet, landing on the balls of his feet.
- Hop ten or more times on both feet in place.

When your child is between the ages of four and five, she will . . .
- Perform a basic—but ineffective—gallop.
- Use her arms and trunk to balance when hopping.
- Execute one to five hops on her preferred foot for a distance of 6 feet.
- Perform a one-footed, uncoordinated skip.

When your child is between the ages of five and six, he will . . .
- Hop eight to twelve times on either foot.
- Begin to alternate feet in skipping.
- Hop 16 feet on one foot easily.
- Gallop and skip skillfully by the age of six.

THROWING

When your child is between the ages of two and three, he . . .

- Will want to throw beyond his capabilities of timing and coordination.
- Will throw a ball backward or as little as a few inches forward.
- May lose his balance when throwing a ball.
- Will throw with forearm extension only, with his body facing the target and his feet stationary.
- Will throw a tennis ball 4 to 5 feet, with practice.
- Can learn to throw a beach ball using both hands.

When your child is between the ages of three and four, she will . . .

- Throw a ball frequently, but not accurately.
- Keep her body fixed while throwing.
- Throw without losing her balance.
- Use her arms to initiate throwing action.
- Move her body in a forward/backward pattern while throwing.
- Throw a large ball 6 feet using both hands.

When your child is between the ages of four and five, he will . . .

- Still use a forward/backward body movement while throwing.
- Still use his arm to initiate his throw.
- Begin to add body rotation to his throwing pattern.
- Keep his feet together while throwing.
- Throw farther.
- Be more accurate in his throw.
- Execute a stronger overhand throw.

When your child is between the ages of five and six, she will . . .

- Begin to transfer her weight on her feet while throwing.
- Step forward with the foot on opposite side of her throwing arm.

CATCHING

When your child is between the ages of two and three, he will . . .

- Chase a ball.
- Attempt to stop a rolling ball with his hands or corral it with his legs when sitting on the floor.
- Respond to an aerial ball with delayed arm movements.
- Need to be told how to position his arms.
- Attempt to catch a large ball thrown from 5 feet away, using his arms and body.
- May close his eyes while attempting to catch the ball.

When your child is between the ages of three and four, she will . . .

- Use her hands and arms as a single unit while attempting to corral the ball against her body.
- Attempt to catch a large ball, using a "basket catch" (upper body leaning forward, knees straight, elbows bent at sides of body, hands together with palms up in front of her body so that her arms form a basket)—but the ball may fall out of her arms.
- Catch a large ball with her arms stiffly extended forward.
- Attempt to catch a small ball with her arms stiffly extended forward.
- Exhibit a fear reaction, turning her head away and perhaps closing her eyes, when a ball is thrown to her.

When your child is between the ages of four and five, he will . . .

- Use his hands more than his arms in catching large balls.
- Catch a large ball thrown from 5 feet away with his arms flexed at the elbows.
- Make an effort to judge the position at which the ball will land.
- Catch large and small balls with his arms flexed and his elbows in front of his body.

When your child is between the ages of five and six, she will . . .

- Use her hands more than arms in catching small balls.
- Judge the trajectory better than at four years, but not always successfully.
- Attempt one-handed catches.
- Catch both large and small balls with her elbows at the sides of her body.
- Catch a large playground ball bounced to her.
- Catch small balls using only her hands.

CLIMBING

When your child is between the ages of two and three, she will . . .
- Love to climb and will climb anywhere.
- Climb on and off a small hobby horse without support.
- Walk upstairs with support, one foot following the other, placing both feet on tread.
- Descend stairs by creeping backward on her knees.

When your child is between the ages of three and four, he will . . .
- Begin to show proficiency climbing on jungle gyms and slides.
- Walk up a short flight of stairs without support, alternating feet.
- Descend stairs without support, one foot following the other and placing both feet on each tread.

When your child is between the ages of four and five, she will . . .
- Descend a long stairway with support, alternating feet.
- Descend a short stairway without support, alternating feet.
- Ascend a large ladder, alternating feet.
- Descend a small ladder, alternating feet.

When your child is between the ages of five and six, he will . . .
- Descend a large ladder, alternating feet.
- Descend a long stairway without support, alternating feet.
- Have mastered ascending skills.

STRIKING, KICKING

When your child is between the ages of two and three, he will . . .

- Strike an object with a bat or stick occasionally, while facing the object and swinging vertically.
- Use very little body movement (other than arm movement) during striking, with his feet remaining stationary.
- Sometimes lose his balance when kicking.
- Kick with his leg straight and little body movement.
- Walk to a ball and kick on command.

When your child is between the ages of three and four, she will . . .

- Have less difficulty in contacting a ball that is thrown under-handed than overhanded.
- Begin to rotate her hips and shoulders when striking.
- Keep her feet together and stationary when striking.
- Begin to swing a bat horizontally.
- Flex her knee on the backward lift of kick.
- Balance her leg movement with her arms held up.

When your child is between the ages of four and five, he will . . .

- Have greater backward and forward swing of his leg with definite arm opposition during the kick.
- Kick a ball on the run.
- Stand to the side of an object and swing in a horizontal plane.

When your child is between the ages of five and six, she will . . .

- Kick a ball, balancing on her opposite foot.
- Kick a soccer ball through the air 8 feet.
- Use a mature kicking pattern, kicking *through* the ball.
- Rotate her trunk and hips and shift her body during striking.

Further Reading

Arnwine, Bonnie (2005). *Starting Sensory Integration Therapy: Fun Activities That Won't Destroy Your Home!* Arlington, TX: Sensory World.

Dennison, Paul E., and Gail E. Dennison (1992). *Brain Gym: Simple Activities for Whole Brain Learning.* Glendale, CA: Edu-Kinesthetics.

Healy, Jane M., Ph.D. (2010). *Different Learners: Identifying, Preventing, and Treating Your Child's Learning Problems.* New York: Simon & Schuster.

Henry, Diana (2008). Tool Chest series of handbooks, including *Tool Chest for Teachers, Parents and Students*; *SI Tools for Teens: Strategies to Promote Sensory Processing*; and *Tools for Tots: Sensory Strategies for Toddlers and Preschoolers.* Glendale, AZ: Henry OT Services. www.ateachabout.com.

Kasser, Susan L. (1995). *Inclusive Games: Movement Fun for Everyone!* Champaign, IL: Human Kinetics.

Kelly, Marguerite (Reissued 2002). *Marguerite Kelly's Family Almanac: A Helpful Guide to Navigating Through the Everyday Issues of Modern Life.* New York: Fireside.

Kranowitz, Carol S. (2006). *The Out-of-Sync Child Has Fun: Activities for Kids with Sensory Processing Disorder,* revised. New York: Perigee.

———— (2005). *The Out-of-Sync Child: Recognizing and Coping with Sensory Processing Disorder,* revised. New York: Perigee.

————— (2002). *Getting Kids in Sync: Sensory-Motor Activities to Help Children Develop Body Awareness and Integrate Their Senses* (video). Arlington, TX: Sensory World.

————— (1995). *101 Activities for Kids in Tight Spaces.* New York: St. Martin's.

McCall, Renée M., and Craft, Diane H. (2000). *Moving with a Purpose: Developing Programs for Preschoolers of All Abilities.* Champaign, IL: Human Kinetics.

Miller, Karen (1999). *Simple Steps: Developmental Activities for Infants, Toddlers, and Two-Year-Olds.* Beltsville, MD: Gryphon House.

Sher, Barbara (2006). *Attention Games: 101 Fun, Easy Games That Help Kids Learn to Focus.* San Francisco: Jossey-Bass.

————— (2009). *Early Intervention Play: Joyful Social and Motor Games for Children with Autism Spectrum and Sensory Processing Disorders.* San Francisco: Jossey-Bass.

Sumner, Christine (2008). *I Can Be: A Child's Whimsical Introduction to Yoga.* Illustrated by Kirk Salopek. Greensburg, PA: Q & J Bird Press.

Stokes, Beverly (2002). *Amazing Babies: Essential Movement for Your Baby in the First Year.* Toronto: Move Alive Media.

Wilson, Debra E., and Heiniger-White, Margot C. (2000). *S'cool Moves for Learning: Enhance Learning Through Self-Regulation Activities.* Shasta, CA: Integrated Learner Press.

Index of In-Sync Activities

▼

N-SYNC ACTIVITIES ARE divided into three groups:

- Beginner—skills of a typical preschooler
- Intermediate—skills of a typical primary school child
- Advanced—skills of a typical elementary school child

Within the three groups, the activities are alphabetized.

We hope you will use these groupings purely as guidelines. Feel free to explore activities from all levels. An "Advanced" child may enjoy and benefit from some of the earlier-level activities, and your "Beginner" child may surprise you with his pleasure and success when digging into higher-level activities.

Page	Beginner Activity	Equipment (Optional Items in Parentheses)
61	Amazing Delivery Kid	Groceries
62	Balloon Buffoon	Balloon
64	Bouncing Baby	Large ball

Page	Beginner Activity	Equipment (Optional Items in Parentheses)
66	Bye, Bye Bubbles	Bubbles, telephone book, paper towel tube (toothpicks)
68	Car Seat Scramble	Car seat
70	Flashlight Tag	Flashlight
72	Good Night, Flashlight!	Two flashlights, colored cellophane
74	Gopher	(Metronome)
76	Hug Roll	Gym mat, mattress, or carpet
78	If I Had a Hammer	Egg carton, foam block, golf tees, mallet (nails, toy hammer)
80	Opposites Attract	
82	Pillow Pile	Plenty of pillows (ball)
84	Red Cup, Blue Cup	Two plastic cups
86	Scootie Cutie	Scooter board (tape, obstacles, rope)
88	Superkid	Gym mat, mattress, or carpet
90	Wheelbarrow	

Page	Intermediate Activity	Equipment (Optional Items in Parentheses)
95	Angel Wings	(Metronome)
97	Arm Circles	
99	Back Drawing	
100	Ball Bounce	Ball, tape (metronome)
102	Bus Driver	Bicycle tube (paper plate or small hoop)
104	Can't Tap Me	
106	Cat Balance Sequence	(Metronome)
108	Chalkboard Circle	Chalkboard and chalk, or paper and crayon (telephone book)

Page	Intermediate Activity	Equipment (Optional Items in Parentheses)
110	Drumroll, Please	Sound makers, for example, rhythm sticks, drum, shaker, sand blocks
112	Eye Spy	Chalkboard and chalk, or poster board and crayon
115	Flashlight Focus	Two flashlights (metronome)
117	Flip Flop	Gym mat, mattress, or carpet
119	Follow the Feather	Feathers
121	Heads Up, Toes Down	Xylophone or keyboard
123	Hip, Hip, Hooray!	Gym mat, mattress, or carpet
125	Keyboard Tales	Piano or keyboard, storybooks
128	Look Ma, No Hands!	Paper plate (obstacles and tape)
130	Make-a-Ball	Ping-Pong or golf ball, rubber bands
132	Newspaper Crumple	Newspaper (laundry basket)
134	Nose to Knee	Gym mat, mattress, or carpet (metronome)
136	Paper Plate Play	Two paper plates (tape, small obstacles, metronome)
138	Penny Pass	Penny, two chairs (metronome)
140	Pipe Cleaner Poke	Pipe cleaners (metronome)
142	Reach for the Sky	Gym mat, mattress, or carpet (metronome)
144	Rolling Log	Two beanbags
146	Roundabout	Chalkboard and chalk, or paper and crayon; toy car (beanbag)
148	Shape Rain	Four to fifty assorted shapes in four different colors, music
150	Shoulder Shrug	(Metronome)
152	Singing String	Fishing line, piece of wood, lacing bead
154	Tap Me Silly	

Page	Intermediate Activity	Equipment (Optional Items in Parentheses)
156	Tummy on the Ball	Gym mat, mattress, or carpet; therapy ball
158	Tweeze and Spell	Alphabet noodles, tweezers, glue, construction paper
160	Wake Up, Arms!	Chair
162	Walk the Plank	Masking tape (beanbags, blocks, or balloon)
164	Watch Your Hands Creep	Gym mat, mattress, or carpet; tape (metronome)

Page	Advanced Activity	Equipment (Optional Items in Parentheses)
169	Clock Wise	Analog clock, chalkboard and chalk, sticker
172	Follow the Bug	Flashlight, chair, wall
174	How Many Steps?	Two beanbags, washcloths, coins, or pebbles to use as markers
176	Jumping Arrows	Minitrampoline, chalkboard and chalk, or poster board and marker
178	Marvelous Marionettes	Metronome, numbered stickers
180	Roll-a-Path	Tape
182	Tick, Tock, Body Clock	Chalk or tape, and beanbags or other markers
184	Write Through Me	Chalkboard and chalk, or paper and pencil or crayon
186	Zany Name Walk	

Activities Particularly Good for . . .

▼

BY IN-SYNC COMPONENT

Balance
- Ball Bounce, 100
- Bouncing Baby, 64
- Cat Balance Sequence, 106
- Hug Roll, 76
- Nose to Knee, 134
- Superkid, 88
- Tap Me Silly, 154
- Tummy on the Ball, 156
- Walk the Plank, 162

Bilateral Coordination
- Angel Wings, 95
- Arm Circles, 97
- Ball Bounce, 100
- Bouncing Baby, 64
- Bye, Bye Bubbles, 66
- Good Night, Flashlight!, 72
- Gopher, 74

- Heads Up, Toes Down, 121
- Make-a-Ball, 130
- Superkid, 88

Body Awareness
- Follow the Feather, 119
- Hip, Hip, Hooray!, 123
- Look Ma, No Hands!, 128
- Nose to Knee, 134
- Reach for the Sky, 142
- Roll-a-Path, 180
- Shoulder Shrug, 150
- Tap Me Silly, 154

Directionality
- Clock Wise, 169
- Jumping Arrows, 176
- Keyboard Tales, 125
- Penny Pass, 138

BY TIME AND PLACE

When You Have Time to Prepare

Index

▼

vestibular processing
  importance of, 10, 12, 17, 23–24, 31
  activities particularly good for, 209
vision/visual processing skills
  importance of, xviii, 6, 9–10, 12–
    13, 15–21, 23–27, 35–36, 114
  activities particularly good for, 209

walking, 191
writing, xviii, 7, 9, 12, 15–18,
  24–27, 32

About the Authors

Carol Kranowitz, a teacher at St. Columba's Nursery School in Washington, DC, for twenty-five years, observed many "out-of-sync" preschoolers. These children were uncomfortable or clumsy in such ordinary activities as walking across the playground, holding hands to play circle games, or going through obstacle courses. To help these anxious children become more competent at work and play, Carol studied a common disability called sensory processing disorder (SPD). SPD is a developmental problem causing difficulty in interpreting and using sensory messages—such as sensations of touch, balance, and movement—to function smoothly in daily life.

In the 1980s, Carol and an occupational therapist began screening preschoolers for SPD. They guided children with probable SPD into occupational therapy, the primary treatment for this disorder. They steered other children with perceptual motor problems (and possible

SPD) into purposeful physical activities, best found at organizations such as Joye Newman's Kids Moving Company. Joye and Carol met and have been buddies ever since.

In 1995, Carol earned her master's degree in education and human development at George Washington University. She created a course of study about her special interest in sensory processing and turned her thesis into a book, *The Out-of-Sync Child: Recognizing and Coping with Sensory Processing Disorder* (Perigee), which was published in 1998 and revised in 2005. This reader-friendly book that makes SPD understandable to parents and teachers has sold more than 600,000 copies. The sequel, *The Out-of-Sync Child Has Fun: Activities for Kids with SPD* (Perigee), was published in 2003 and revised in 2006. It has sold more than 225,000 copies. In her other books and DVDs and in national and international workshops, Carol explains to parents, educators, and other professionals how sensory issues play out and suggests enjoyable strategies for addressing them at home and school.

Carol is a board member of STAR (Sensory Therapies and Research) Center. Her website is www.out-of-sync-child.com.

Joye Newman is a perceptual motor therapist. Perceptual motor therapy (PMT) provides integrated movement experiences that develop and enhance gross motor, fine motor, and visual perception abilities. In 1979, Joye, like Carol, earned her master's degree in education and human development from GWU, with a specialty in perceptual motor development. Integrating studies in behavioral optometry, occupational therapy, and psychology into her graduate work, she developed her unique method of PMT.

Shortly after receiving her degree, Joye founded and continues to direct a popular organization called Kids Moving Company (KMC). She began KMC because she was concerned that many kids were not encouraged to move—in fact, many kids were discouraged from moving—at home and school. She wanted to provide a place for children to move, play, and think in a developmentally appropriate environment. At the studio, KMC offered fun and functional activities, birthday parties, and perceptual motor therapy to children with and without special needs. In 2007, Joye closed the studio to focus on in-school programs, individual evaluations, and consultations with parents to help them understand how they can help their children become more confident and competent in everything they do.

Joye was a founding member and the original education chair of WISER (Washington Independent Services for Educational Resources); a cofounder of the Jewish Primary Day School of Washington, DC; and the early childhood special needs consultant for the Board of Jewish Education. She lectures on school readiness, creative movement, and perceptual motor development, and she consults to area preschools, helping them develop and refine their movement programs. Her website is www.kidsmovingco.com.

When Carol and Joye met many years ago, they realized that they share the same sense of humor, the same politics, and the ability to know what the other is thinking and saying. They also share the same mission—to get kids In Sync with the world. Long before they sat down to start writing, their work with children was, in fact, this book in action.

To learn more, visit www.in-sync-child.com
and follow Growing an In-Sync Child on Facebook.